SIMPLE SOLUTIONS

SIMPLE SOLUTIONS

How "Enterprise Project
Management" Supported Harvard
Pilgrim Health Care's Journey
from Near Collapse to #1

Lisa A. DiTullio

iUniverse, Inc.
New York Lincoln Shanghai

Simple Solutions
How "Enterprise Project Management"Supported Harvard
Pilgrim Health Care's Journey from Near Collapse to #1

Copyright © 2007 by Lisa A. DiTullio

iUniverse books may be ordered through booksellers
or by contacting:

iUniverse
2021 Pine Lake Road, Suite 100
Lincoln, NE 68512
www.iuniverse.com
1-800-Authors (1-800-288-4677)

Because of the dynamic nature of the Internet, any Web addresses
or links contained in this book may have changed
since publication and may no longer be valid.

The views expressed in this work are solely those of the author and do
not necessarily reflect the views of the publisher, and the publisher hereby
disclaims any responsibility for them.

ISBN: 978-0-595-46110-3 (pbk)
ISBN: 978-0-595-70069-1 (cloth)
ISBN: 978-0-595-90410-5 (ebk)

Printed in the United States of America

Dedicated to my parents, for their unwavering love and support.

To my husband George, for his sound guidance, endless encouragement, and abundant affection. To my children Kaleigh and Geoff, for constantly reminding me what is important in life; and to my step-daughters Linsday, Genny and Jill, for their inquisitiveness and acceptance.

Table of Contents

Acknowledgements

This book could not have happened without the contributions, guidance, and counsel from the following individuals: Heidi Aylward, Charlie Baker, Lisa Barnstein, Suzanne Bates, Susan Bentcourt, John Bonanno, Robert Buttrick, Bruce Bullen, Jack Calhoun, Melissa Clark, Vicki Coates, David Cochran, Mary Ellen Conlon, Deb Hicks, Ron Hill, Mark Jorjorian, Mary Joyce, Steve Kadish, Scott Kessloff, Ken Lizotte, Chris Miller, Deborah Norton, Ron Parello, Suzy Park, Laura Peabody, Mike Plunkett, Parviz Rad, Armando Rodrigues, Dave Segal, Alan Slobodnik, Bob Sullivan, Jim Thrasivoulos, Meg Tiedemann, Sandy Trantina, Steve Trotsky, Kate Victory, Neal Whitten and Gina Westcott.

Introduction: The Harvard Pilgrim Health Care Story

All organizations want success, but none can achieve it without encountering obstacles along the way. For some organizations, the gap between promises made and delivery of those promises is too large, forcing them to fall victim to business disaster. The key is to master the skills that prevent disasters—and project management skills are an essential part of this skill set.

This book explains how project management methodology has supported Harvard Pilgrim Health Care's remarkable journey from being placed in state receivership in 2000 to being named the "Number One Health Plan in America" in 2004, 2005 and 2006 (by *US News & World Report* and the National Committee for Quality Assurance*). It recounts the creation and evolution of Harvard Pilgrim's Project Management Office and the roles of key stakeholders across the organization to successfully support Enterprise Project Management. Most importantly, this book is also about how project management translates to good business management in a disciplined, efficient way—and how you can apply this in your own organization.

In 1995, two prominent, Boston-based health maintenance organizations (HMOs), each nationally recognized for quality and service excellence, merged to become the largest health plan in New England. Harvard Community Health Plan and Pilgrim Health Care combined

---

*   Harvard Pilgrim Health Care was named the nation's top-rated health plan for member satisfaction and quality of care in 2004 by the National Committee for Quality Assurance (NCQA). In 2005 and 2006, Harvard Pilgrim was named the top-rated health plan according to a joint ranking of commercial plans by *U.S.News & World Report* and NCQA. NCQA is a private, non-profit organization dedicated to improving health care quality. "America's Best Health Plans" is a trademark of *U.S.News & World Report*.

their operations into Harvard Pilgrim Health Care, a 1 million-member health plan serving four New England states.

Harvard Community Health Plan, based in Brookline, Massachusetts, was founded in 1969 as a staff model HMO. Harvard had its own salaried doctors who treated patients at centers around Greater Boston. Pilgrim Health Care was founded in 1981 with a goal of organizing doctors who wanted to remain as independent practitioners. Both not-for-profit entities, they had a strong desire to improve the health of society; their mission was built on three cornerstones—service, quality, and innovation. For employers, the merged organization would offer one-stop shopping for their health insurance needs.

In 1996, Harvard Pilgrim began combining its separate health insurance products and marketed a combined product—Harvard Pilgrim HMO—as a way to get employers and members used to the idea of dealing with one company. Over a period of two years, the organization phased out its legacy products and switched its members to new, combined health products. While this was occurring, Harvard Pilgrim was also working to integrate "back room" operations while maintaining high-level service delivery to its customers.

After years of finding ways to cut the cost of health care, managed care health plans were being hit by a hard reality in the late 1990s: expenses were rising faster than plans could find places to trim them. New drugs, technology, and large numbers of aging baby boomers were hurting profits. Costs were exceeding what the industry had expected, forcing insurers to hike premiums to compensate. Environmental changes were causing some insurers to rethink some common assumptions and come up with new ways to deliver quality care at affordable prices. Harvard Pilgrim was not immune to these changes.

Provider networks were expanding, forcing health plans to contract with more hospitals and physicians in order to offer consumer choice. But offering choice came with a price: additional contract negotiations with providers limited health plans' ability to negotiate deep discounts with hospitals and doctors in exchange for steering patients to them. And to make things more difficult, the managed care tools previously used to reduce costs were being taken away by market pressures and regulatory changes. The shifting landscape forced local and national

HMOs back to the drawing board to update their assumptions about managed care's biggest asset—its ability to control costs.

In November 1997, the multi-specialty physician practice that acted as the hub for Harvard Community Health Plan's original staff model split from Harvard Pilgrim Health Care to form their own non-profit group practice. In 1999, the group practice, which consisted of 14 regional health centers and was run by over 900 physicians, nurses and clinicians, chose a new name to further emphasize their independent status: Harvard Vanguard Medical Associates. This break was quite symbolic for both parties; it met Harvard Vanguard Medical Associates' desire to obtain true independence, allowing the practice to broaden its contract beyond Harvard Pilgrim Health Care and grow their patient base. The separation also gave Harvard Pilgrim Health Care the opportunity to break free of their HMO brand and to re-establish themselves as a full-service benefits organization—a way for HPHC to expand their membership base through broad product and network offerings. Both parties viewed the disunion as favorable for future success.

At the same time, Harvard Pilgrim was experiencing problems managing their multiple operating systems acquired through the merger. By 1999, these systems were still not speaking to one another and indications of problems began to surface. Doctors and hospitals were becoming increasingly frustrated with Harvard Pilgrim's inability to pay them on time for seeing patients. In fact, the problem became so severe that some physician groups were sending HPHC's members elsewhere to get care. Some providers were sure the delays in payment were a result of computer glitches; other providers were less understanding—they believed the delays in payments were blatant acts of bad faith and plain incompetence.

In spite of HPHC's struggles, the company continued to achieve success. In *Newsweek's* September 28, 1998 issue, Harvard Pilgrim was named the top health plan in the US, a welcome accolade for any HMO, given the many competitive challenges. The ratings are determined by looking at how health plans keep members healthy, manage chronic conditions, and treat acute illness. In the same year, a J.D. Power and Associates survey named HPHC the best HMO in the

Boston area, based on a survey of 3,500 Massachusetts HMO members. The award rates HMOs on patients' opinions on the choice of physicians, confidence in the plan, and the quality of care they receive from plan physicians.

However, these awards were not enough to sustain Harvard Pilgrim Health Care. The struggle to mesh differing cultures and operational systems was becoming even more difficult. In late 1998, HPHC eliminated over 100 jobs, including a number of high-level positions, to deal with unexpectedly large financial losses. The organization, which at the time employed over 4,500 people, lost $22.2 million in the first three quarters of 1998 on revenue of nearly $2 billion. To make up for losses, Harvard Pilgrim began to realign and focus resources to operate more efficiently.

In May 1999, Harvard Pilgrim's CEO and CFO abruptly resigned amid financial and operational turmoil. The organization posted a $94 million loss from operations in 1998. Once again, its fragmented computer systems were partly to blame for its larger-than-expected losses.

When Charles D. Baker joined Harvard Pilgrim in mid-1999, the organization was losing $225 million. The organization was in operational and financial crisis—and near collapse. Staff resided within strict functional boundaries, not speaking across business units, yet everyone blamed everyone else for the organization's woes. People no longer had a sense of shared purpose and efficient processes were no longer in place. Staff were still wedded to their legacy organizations; they were unable to see the bigger picture that meant survival.

The pressure was on for Baker and his team; Harvard Pilgrim was hemorrhaging, and needed immediate solutions. HPHC's new leader needed to give people hope. HPHC staff had to believe that the new leadership team would be aspirational; would listen to each other and to the rank and file; would make adjustments when circumstances dictated; would keep people informed; and would help people see how what they did fit into the overall scheme of things. When asked about the daunting task ahead of him, Baker replied candidly, "Do I think I can do this? I don't know the answer to that one. I certainly think

I've seen this movie before. But this is going to be a lot of work. I am definitely smart enough to know that nothing is a sure thing."

In 1999, HPHC pursued a targeted, aggressive plan to turn the organization around in 2000. Known as the "150-Day Campaign," the plan commenced in August and ended in December. It focused on five areas:

1. The organization consolidated the management structure to create one organization with single points of accountability. Some people were brought in from the outside while others were promoted from within.

2. HPHC outsourced their information technology (IT) operations and claims processing activities to Perot Systems, the largest operator of AMISYS benefits administration and claims processing platforms in the US. (AMISYS is HPHC's primary claims payment and eligibility operating platform).

3. HPHC revamped their pharmacy benefit, moving quickly to a three-tier formulary to control escalating costs associated with drug utilization, and changed pharmacy vendors to further enhance administrative savings.

4. HPHC gradually exited the Rhode Island marketplace, where they had about 1,000 employees and about 200,000 members. This was perhaps one of the most difficult decisions, as Rhode Island represented 20 percent of HPHC's membership, but almost half of the operating loss.

5. HPHC re-contracted their provider network in 90 days, a process that typically takes years. The organization accomplished this through termination of complex, customized provider agreements that were nearly impossible to configure and support, replacing them with agreements that were simpler, standardized, and came with performance guarantees from HPHC.

This new discipline and these activities, which supported execution of the turnaround plan, were the beginning stages of a project management discipline for HPHC.

Receivership

Having implemented the initial 150-day turnaround plan, HPHC received a shattering blow on January 4, 2000. The Commonwealth of Massachusetts placed HPHC under state supervision through a court order. The court order was filed in response to ballooning 1999 losses, which eventually totaled approximately $227 million. Under the court order, the state insurance commissioner assumed oversight for financial operations to help HPHC avoid bankruptcy and achieve financial stability.

The move was made to protect HPHC's members and their ability to receive care. According to Thomas Reilly, Massachusetts' Attorney General at the time, the State sought this action to make sure Harvard Pilgrim's clients would have continuity of medical care. Reilly said in a *Boston Globe* article that the State wanted to make sure that legal measures were in place, that business would continue as usual, and that doctors, patients, and hospitals should not panic or overreact. The relationship between Tom Reilly and Harvard Pilgrim Health Care would prove to be a positive one.

As receivership took place, membership continued to plummet. For many employers, HPHC was no longer a trusted organization to purchase health coverage from; accounts and members were quickly leaving the plan to obtain insurance elsewhere. Many hospitals around New England worried about how the possible downfall of a major health insurance plan would affect their own bottom lines.

HPHC maintained its course and the turnaround plan began to produce results. HPHC posted profitable third and fourth quarters in 2000. This was nearly on target with what the HMO originally forecasted, and was the start of continued financial gains.

By mid-2001, HPHC's operating and financial performance had improved. The company reported a first quarter net gain of almost $4 million; Member and Provider Call Center metrics were back to peak performance levels, suggesting HPHC was once again able to provide high-touch customer support—impressive, considering the circumstances. Yet, HPHC's battle was far from over. Members continued to leave the plan; membership bottomed out at 730,000 in mid-2001.

In early June 2001, Charlie Baker told his management staff HPHC needed to stay focused and not be complacent or slow to make decisions. The work ahead during the coming six months was critically important, not just for the remainder of the year, but to set the stage for success in the following year as well. "January 2002 will be another big test for us."

HPHC's focus began to pay off over the next few years. In 2002, HPHC introduced *Best Buy HMO* to Massachusetts employers, a new product that has many of the same features as traditional HMO plan designs, but offers lower premiums. HPHC was the first health plan in Massachusetts to offer such product designs and now has over 120,000 lives enrolled in their Massachusetts product. Their innovative efforts generated products which offer comprehensive health benefits at more affordable rates by introducing additional cost-sharing features like deductibles, coinsurance, or higher co-payments for certain covered services. The products were designed to address rising costs while continuing to provide quality coverage. The new product line allowed employees to save on their premiums every month and have peace of mind knowing they could receive quality care. HPHC then introduced similar PPO and POS product designs and expanded the new offerings in New Hampshire and Maine, strengthening their northern New England presence.

In 2005, HPHC expanded their product portfolio again by offering *Best Buy HSA PPO*. The new High Deductible Health Plan (HDHP) is a health insurance product whose benefit design is governed by the US Department of the Treasury and was created to help control escalating health care premiums. The products are designed with a deductible, increasing members' out-of-pocket exposure. A tax-favored savings vehicle, known as a Health Savings Account (HSA), is attached to the new HDHP line of products. The HSA enables participants to pay for health care services not covered by insurance or other sources. Similar to an Individual Retirement Account (IRA), the HSA has added flexibility that allows participants to withdraw money pre-retirement with no penalty for qualified medical expenses. HPHC was successful in launching the new products in both Massachusetts and New Hampshire, allowing them to retain a strong position in a highly competitive market.

The Company Passed the Test

In June 2006, the Massachusetts Supreme Judicial Court officially released Harvard Pilgrim Health Care from any further oversight by state government relative to the organization's past financial troubles. This achievement was made far more quickly than most outsiders had predicted. No health organization had ever been ordered by the Massachusetts courts into a temporary receivership; and in 2000, the media speculation about HPHC's future had been grim.

The good news is this: the turnaround plan worked. Not only did Harvard Pilgrim work itself back from the brink of financial disaster, but it also went on to win a number of prestigious awards as both a health plan and as an employer. In 2006, Harvard Pilgrim Health Care closed the year with 996,000 members and posted a $70 million net gain.

Today, the organization's mission remains the same—to improve the health of the people it serves and the health of society. Harvard Pilgrim now provides health insurance coverage to over 1 million members, primarily in Massachusetts, Maine, and New Hampshire. In response to employer requests to provide coverage for their employees living and working across the US, HPHC entered into a partnership with United Healthcare, and now offers products and services to employers' office locations anywhere in the country. HPHC's product portfolio and funding arrangements meet the needs of virtually any employer, regardless of size or location. They recently launched www. LetsTalkHealthCare.org, an interactive issues-focused site that features a blog hosted by Charlie Baker, as well as a resource center providing industry news.

Harvard Pilgrim Health Care realized success by being effective in selecting the "right" projects and by being efficient in delivering on the action plan. Over the years, HPHC has perfected its ability to execute its business plans through processes and tools that allow people to get the work done simply and quickly. Establishing a project management culture over a period of time has allowed HPHC to deliver on priority work in an organized and results-oriented manner.

Charlie Baker agrees. "Project management metrics are every bit as important as call center metrics, new sales, member retention, and the other, more commonly understood tools companies use to measure their performance. Over time, success is driven by two things—your ability to compete day-to-day in serving your customers, and your ability to change with the market, to meet the new needs and expectations of your constituents. Strong project management is critical to delivering on both of these objectives, and it's especially important to the second one. Being there, on time and on budget, with the next new thing, is often what separates great organizations from mediocre ones."

Today, Harvard Pilgrim Health Care is the "Number One Health Plan in America," according to a joint ranking in 2006 by *US News & World Report* and the National Committee for Quality Assurance (NCQA). HPHC has led the country for member satisfaction and quality of care for three years in a row. And for the last five years in a row, the *Boston Business Journal* has named HPHC one of the "Best Places to Work." In March 2007, JD Power & Associates conducted its inaugural National Health Insurance Plans Satisfaction Study; Harvard Pilgrim Health Care ranked highest in the Northeast region and had the highest score in the country.

Harvard Pilgrim's vision is to be the most trusted and respected name in health care. They hope to distinguish themselves from the competition by delivering a unique consumer experience in a world where consumers have increasing responsibility for their own health-care decisions among more product choices. The world of health care continues to change, and Harvard Pilgrim Health Care seems ready for the challenge—due in no small part to its project management skills.

This book will show you how to gain and apply similar project management skills in your organization. You will find simple practices, techniques, and tools, all which have been tested and proven at Harvard Pilgrim Health Care—and which can be easily adopted in your organization.

Chapter 1

Getting Started: Project Management Organization Basics

Any intelligent fool can make things bigger and more complex ... It takes a touch of genius—and a lot of courage to move in the opposite direction ...

Albert Einstein

Profitability. Success. Customer Loyalty. These are words often used to describe bottom-line goals for business organizations. At Harvard Pilgrim Health Care, these words are accompanied by other ones—Understandable, Timely, Accurate, Responsive, Reliable and Predictable. However, when it comes time for organizations to execute on the business plan, too often we hear Delay, Restart, Over-Budget, Under-Resourced and Cancel.

How can an organization get better at delivering on its goals and objectives? One way is to establish a strategic, enterprise-wide Project Management Office (PMO) model.

If properly managed, a PMO can successfully support tactical execution of a strategic vision—and a whole lot more.

Whether your organization is in crisis or simply desires to remain competitive, your business plan requires multiple phases over periods of time. Your plan may include tactics for achieving financial success. Another component may involve cultural change within the organization, while another may address new product development. All phases require a set of tactics for delivering on the plan. These tactics translate into projects, which are complex, demanding, and messy. Projects are

1

critical building blocks in achieving an organization's strategic plan. A PMO seamlessly choreographs all the moving parts. A strategic project management office is about building tools, methods, and techniques for project *and* business success. If you build a PMO with this goal in mind, and your plan to establish and run a PMO maintains an eye for simplicity, your organization can reap huge rewards. In fact, over time, a PMO can facilitate and support organizational processes well beyond projects to further enhance overall business success.

Establishing a project management culture allows organizations to speed up decision-making, improve accountability, understand interdependent work efforts, and enhance overall communication across the organization. Project management does not need to be complex or complicated to offer value. In fact, keeping it simple allows companies to develop project management competencies that, over time, become part of the organizational culture.

At Harvard Pilgrim Health Care, the Enterprise Project Management Office (EPMO) staff has a favorite phrase that supports their desire to maintain simplicity: "In spite of all the flavors offered, vanilla is still our favorite."

Project management puts processes and tools in place that allow companies to get work done efficiently. It allows businesses to communicate priority projects (the agenda), apply consistent project management practices (the methodology), and monitor project progress (the pulse). The PMO is the conduit for making this happen—up, down, and across the organization.

Establishing and maintaining a PMO does not require large investments. Amazingly enough, the power of a successful PMO does not come from its size. HPHC's PMO is a small but mighty army of five; four project managers and one director. The unit successfully supports a corporate portfolio of approximately 40 large, cross-functional projects—the projects which are most important to HPHC's future success—each year. Two staff members act as full-time consultants; they provide general support, facilitation, guidance, and education to project managers who are responsible for managing the 40 large, priority projects. The other two project managers float between the consultant/support role and the project manager function. In other words, they either support a project manager, or actually act as the project manager, based upon resource needs. The director manages the unit, as well as acts on a number of senior executive committees, all responsible for defining and managing the organization's future strategic direction.

One of the keys to HPHC's success in recent years has been their ability to scope, start, and finish projects in a timely and cost-effective manner, thereby adding value to their organization, customers, and trading partners. The work of their project managers is successful, for the most part, because they take the set-up process seriously, try to make adjustments when needed, and strive to keep the work focused and "in scope." Project management at HPHC is successful because it is endorsed from the top of the organization and was created specifically to ensure that corporate initiatives involving multiple departments are pursued efficiently and on time.

Why is this so important? When you consider the remarkable story of HPHC's success, keep in mind that the adoption and practice of project management has enabled an organization to turn chaos into calm. Successful project delivery has remedied their multi-system interoperability. Some of HPHC's project successes include: moving from multiple operating systems to one; switching from accepting only paper claims to processing electronic claims submissions; and automating what were once manual processes. The company has leveraged technology to enhance the customer's experience. In other words, HPHC's success is due to more than just luck.

Throughout this book, we will track a specific HPHC project to illustrate the power of project management. This real-life case study will demonstrate how project management tools and processes can work in real time in a real organization to produce real results.

Case Study Introduction

In 2004, HPHC leadership approved a project to assess options associated with changing their fulfillment vendor (for customer materials), in response to increasingly poor performance by the current vendor and low customer satisfaction. The journey began in October 2004 when a request for information (RFI) proposal was sent to various vendors, including a late entry vendor. The project team evaluated all vendors (a total of six candidates). Vendor selection was based upon RFI information, face-to-face vendor meetings at HPHC, and the ability of vendor candidates to meet HPHC's business requirements.

Once vendor selection was completed, a cross-functional team was formed to assist with the implementation of the fulfillment initiative. Over the following five months, the project team accelerated implementation timelines and worked with three vendors to review and understand HPHC business and technical requirements, establish service level agreements, redesign data files and reporting needs, re-design member book covers, develop customized print-on-demand post-sale books, negotiate pricing, and negotiate letters of intent and definitive agreements.

With the existing fulfillment vendor's contract set to expire on October 1, 2005, the project team was forced to perform under tight timelines with limited resources in order to meet production schedules. On September 12, 2005, the team successfully began to approve production for each initiative, starting with premium bills, Welcome Kits, ID cards, Explanation of Benefits (EOBs) statements, and lastly, Provider checks and reports.

In Chapter 2, we will see how this project was introduced and added to HPHC's corporate agenda as a priority initiative. We will continue to follow its journey from concept to closure, periodically pausing at different checkpoints along its route. Watch for the Vendor Fulfillment project in a variety of places throughout the book, as each contact will expose how HPHC's simple project management practices and tool use supported the project's success.

Find Your Place

A PMO's location in an organization will determine its degree of long-term success. Due to the rapid change to, and cost of, technology, many organizations have historically placed a PMO within their information technology (IT) division. Since a majority of projects reside within the IT shop and are a large source of capital spending, it makes perfect sense to have a PMO oversee technology projects. However, most business plans today include a variety of corporate priorities, many of which reside outside of IT territory.

Interestingly, most organizations do not have a PMO at the enterprise (or corporate) level. So, where does support for the corporate business plan occur? How does the organization know what projects are important? How do senior executives know if they are on track for successful delivery of the business plan? How do business leaders know when to allocate the "right" resources to the "right" initiatives? An Enterprise Project Management Office (EPMO) is an excellent way to support overall business plan success. From this point forward, all references to EMPO or PMO indicate a project management office at the enterprise level.

In recent years, organizations that have installed project management offices have done so in a variety of ways, and as a result, call them by a variety of names. It really doesn't matter if you call it a Project/Program Management Office (PMO) or an Enterprise Project Management Office (EPMO). In fact, you can also have multiple "PMOs" in your organization and still be effective. (It is very common for IT divisions to have their own PMO, for example, for the above-stated reasons.) The key to success is not what you name it or how many you have—the key is to have one corporate unit, at the enterprise level, to oversee corporate project activities that directly support the corporate business plan.

HPHC has two formal PMOs; one at the enterprise level, the other within the IT Division, managed by outside vendor Perot Systems. The two units have co-existed since 1999 and have no trouble defining their roles and relationships in support of business plan delivery. According to Ron Hill, Perot Systems Client Executive to HPHC, the pathway for success is "born from the teamwork of the EPMO and the IT PMO." Hill believes the strength of the relationship between the two units is visible through the communication between the EPMO, the IT PMO, and the business users. "Everyone must use the same methodology, vernacular, and project tools to reduce the risk of miscommunication."

Hill also believes the success of multiple PMOs existing within HPHC is a result of well-defined roles and responsibilities and the early engagement of all key players. "When we start a project together, you will find not only the business, the EPMO and the IT PMO, you will also find the Business Analysts, Solutions Architects, and Test Architects all at the table from the onset to manage and ensure a measured outcome."

Deborah Norton, HPHC's Chief Information Officer (CIO), agrees. "There's always the risk of lack of clarity about roles when you have multiple PMOs, such as communication issues and turf wars over responsibilities." Norton believes organizations can successfully implement and manage multiple PMOs when the organization has the "right" cultural view. "It starts with the overarching philosophy of serving the business and then an active willingness to work together to provide the best support to the organization."

Norton views the value of the EPMO as being much like that of the air traffic controller at an airport: "I wouldn't fly without one." She thinks that standardization of tool kits, methodologies, etc. offer economies of scale for the organization. She also believes the EPMO has a lifelong role in any organization, "Let's face it, it's a life's work, it is never done, we can always evolve to a better place. That's what we are trying to accomplish with this 'harmonizing' effect."

Where your EPMO resides in your organization will determine its corporate effectiveness and longevity. Many PMOs start out strong, only to fade after a few years due to a lack of executive support. HPHC's EPMO reports directly to the Chief Operating Officer (COO), with a dotted line to the Chief Executive Officer (CEO). Placing the EPMO at this level enables the project management office to establish relationships at all levels of the organization, starting at the top. Harvard Pilgrim's CEO and COO both agree the PMO must reside at this level to be effective. According to CEO Baker, "If it's not sponsored somewhere high up in the organization, it can't create visibility around successes, failures, and near-disasters." Baker believes the PMO's greatest strength is serving as an "honest broker." "There's a lot of learning and helping there, too—but fundamentally, its greatest value is in its ability to tell management what's really going on with its change agenda."

A PMO located at a high level within an organization will receive respect and have clout. It also represents neutrality. When a PMO is a stand-alone unit, reporting to the highest senior executives, it is viewed as non-biased in its intent. The PMO, through a Switzerland-like presence, can unselfishly support the organization's goals without prejudice or self-interest. Regardless of where your PMO resides, one thing is clear: You must have endorsement from the top. Yet, getting this endorsement tends to be the biggest challenge.

Get the Support You Need

It must be remembered that there is nothing more difficult to plan, more doubtful of success, nor more dangerous to manage, than the creation of a new system. For the initiator has the enmity of all who would profit by the preservation of the old institutions and merely lukewarm defenders in those who would gain by the new ones.

Machiavelli

If you have been tapped to establish a PMO in your organization, someone somewhere has recognized the value of project management. Establishing a strong alliance with this individual will be your ticket to success. If the CEO or COO has brought you in, the job of acquiring corporate buy-in will be easier. Teaming up with a senior executive who can rally the troops and help sell the value of project management is your best approach. Spend time with this individual to establish yourself at the executive table. Share your business plan, your vision, and your implementation schedule with your executive sponsor. Present examples of what an EPMO can accomplish; the possibilities are endless. At HPHC, the EPMO resolves resource allocation and resource contention issues, provides technical support to project managers and project stakeholders, identifies over-subscribed subject matter experts, offers meeting facilitation services, and provides consultation services, just to name a few tasks.

When Bruce M. Bullen became Harvard Pilgrim's COO in 1999, the organization was in turmoil. He knew HPHC needed immediate process, discipline, and focus to survive. Bullen recognized the value of project management from his previous role in state government, and quickly endorsed the introduction of project management practices at HPHC.

Bullen notes: "At first merely an emergency mechanism to ensure the success of our corporate turnaround, the HPHC enterprise project management office has evolved into an indispensable piece of our operating model. Shepherding the projects in our annual business plan, our EPMO provides the executive team with timely information on project status and strengthens our ability to meet expectations by supporting the managers who are responsible for implementing our business plan. A healthy organization must change and must also manage the disruption of change—this is where the EPMO comes in."

You must leverage your relationship with your strongest supporters—the believers—to gain acceptance from your entire executive team. Ideally, all executives must believe in the value of project management before you can introduce it to the organization as a whole. At the very least, you must garner senior executive support *while* introducing project management to the entire organization. Without senior executive support, the EPMO will fail, regardless of how clear and defined your plan may be. Identify your allies first, establish a relationship with them, and rely on them to help spread the word. Market your PMO; convince your executive stakeholders of the value of project management.

Dave Segal, Senior Vice President of Customer Service and Market Performance, has been with Harvard Pilgrim Health Care for many years. The concept of project management was not new to him when HPHC established a formal project management methodology. In fact, prior to the establishment of HPHC's PMO, his division used project management to manage many product development and implementation initiatives. However, what really made Segal a believer was observing how HPHC used project management during the turnaround. "When your back is to the wall and resources are limited, the discipline of project management becomes an essential ingredient for success," Segal states.

He believes the HPHC project management tool set, when employed with discipline, allows the company to carefully define and manage project scope, and to carefully manage timeline and resources. Before this approach was introduced, HPHC used project management to guide the work. "As Harvard Pilgrim emerged from its turnaround phase, HPHC continued, and still continues, to use project management as a way to optimally deliver on scope, while managing scarce resources in a competitive environment."

The science of project management adds value to getting the work done efficiently and consistently. The art of project management enhances overall business outcomes. When selling project management to the non-believers, it is sometimes better to not over-promote the technical aspect of project management. Instead, focus on the overall value of project management. Market "project management" to your executive stakeholders as "business management." HPHC uses an "executive project management" model, which combines facility project management, IT/"technical" project management, and advocacy management. Sold as a package, HPHC's EPMO supports overall business success.

A major cause of many failed PMO's is an over-emphasis on the technical aspects of project management. Forcing project management language and technique before an organization is ready is apt to cause organizational revolt. When HPHC initially introduced project management using phrases like work breakdown structure, scope creep, dependencies, critical path, network diagram, and triple constraint, these terms were met with empty stares.

Initially, HPHC needed to relate to staff on a business and logical level rather than a project management professional level. They quickly shifted to alternate conversations like these:

- "All your work is in this box. If you don't document your work in that manner, you can't keep people from adding to the box and you won't be able to manage people's expectations about what is in the box and what you intend to do."

- "Let's document the work that needs to be done by others so that you can do yours."
- "Let's outline our work, noting which items must be done before others; this will help us determine when we can finish."

Once the concepts were used and understood, HPHC could then apply the project management-related terminology and technique.

Bob Sullivan, PMP,* is one of the original members of HPHC's EPMO and was instrumental in helping design and implement Harvard Pilgrim's project management methodology. Considered a maverick in the early days, Sullivan has experienced extraordinary challenges while lobbying for corporate endorsement of project management practice.

"During the turnaround, the organization was faced with the responsibility of successfully completing a myriad of life-saving projects in a condensed time frame with the same discipline, mentality, and culture that had been so ineffective at project work in the past. One of Charlie Baker's principles of change had been to sow the seeds of dissatisfaction with the status quo. He basically told us that we had to change because we had been so ineffective in the past. No sugarcoating. Armed with this knowledge, the organization was ready for a new discipline for project work."

Sullivan believes the PMO's incessant lobbying for project management has paid off. "We now recognize that projects effect necessary change in the organization. Further, our culture has adopted a discipline to perform projects where we own the work, define the work, plan the work, and actively manage that work." That's an enviable state for any organization.

---

*   The PMP credential stands for "Project Management Professional." It is received when an individual meets specific educational and project management experience requirements and agrees to adhere to a code of professional conduct, as defined by the Project Management Institute, a global community dedicated to the growth and development of the project management profession.

Establish an External Network

While it is important to establish strong relationships with senior executives who believe in project management, it is equally important to establish an external network. Seek other PMO leaders in local communities or similar industries who are willing to share best practices. The concept of a PMO is still relatively fresh for many organizations. Individuals who have been selected to establish or manage a project management office are still fairly new to the role. They are hungry to exchange ideas and best practices with colleagues. The time and energy you invest in establishing such a collaboration is well worth it. Many PMO leaders can share experiences, tools and templates without revealing company intelligence or proprietary information.

Seek PMO leaders who come from organizations similar in size and revenue to yours. An organization with twice as much revenue and resources may provide some insight, but will not have experienced similar challenges. Listen closely to what works well and more importantly, what failed. Appreciate the cultural similarities and differences when sharing best practices. What may work well for one company may not work well for yours. Successfully managing a PMO requires 20 percent technical project management expertise and 80 percent intuitive "read" of your organization's culture. Don't push process and technique simply for their own sakes; it will fail. Disbelievers view project management as just a last-ditch effort for troubled companies. But understand that the benefits associated with proactively introducing a project management office now are likely to avert a crisis later.

Who Should Lead the Charge?

Not all project managers make good PMO leaders. Many seasoned, well-trained project managers clearly see the value of good project management practice. A strong project manager can successfully manage a complex project through application of project management techniques and tools. However, a skilled project manager cannot always run a PMO successfully, as the skill set and experience needed to run the PMO goes beyond the technical practice of project management.

A successful PMO leader will understand the business, culture, and politics of an organization. A competent PMO leader will have a seat at the executive table and be viewed as a valuable team player, having established strong relationships throughout the entire organization. Technical know-how and understanding of project management coupled with proficient leadership skills, strong character and integrity is a recipe for long tenure and success. A consummate PMO leader should not focus entirely on technical application of project management practices. The focus on technical application must be applied with an appreciation for organizational pain. Understand and recognize severe organizational pain and apply a plan that integrates alignment with overall business success to address the acute pain.

HPHC's EPMO is a happy marriage between a strong business leader and proficient project managers. The EPMO leader is not a formally trained project manager, but is a successful business leader who understands the industry and who has strong working relationships with all levels across the organization. Certified, experienced project managers who are well-versed in the technical application of project management can balance the equation; this enables the EPMO to serve all corporate needs in support of project management activities.

The Importance of Sequence

When developing your plan to establish a PMO, keep a bias towards action and common sense. Push cost-benefit decisions. Strive to balance organizational priorities and departmental specific needs. Focus on results, money, and time. Think of the PMO as both a tool and a catalyst in getting the job done. Act in an enabling and facilitative way and build key partnerships with business units across the organization.

Building a PMO is like constructing a new building—you need a well-designed, thoughtful plan; a sturdy foundation; collaboration and contribution from many different specialists; and a shared view of the final product. The building does not need to immediately have all comforts and luxuries, but its design must be able to easily accommodate changing needs, variable climates, and have the ability to last over time.

Establishing a PMO for long-term success depends upon completing the right sequence of activities over a long period of time. Always look for corporate discomfort and apply practices, tools, and techniques that reduce or eliminate the pain. (We'll look at examples of corporate pain later in this book.) Establish a common approach, which, over time, prioritizes projects to meet strategic goals, focuses resources to business priorities, enables better and faster decision-making, and improves accountability. Maintain a simple plan; don't get so caught up in the intricacies of project management that you lose sight of why the PMO exists; and never lose sight of the PMO's overall value to the organization.

Design a plan to implement the PMO in sequential phases. Never let the perfect be the enemy of the good. Establishing a PMO plan requires flexibility and adjustment; never expect the plan to be right the first time—it will always require tweaking and adjustment. Running a PMO is a journey; its work is never finished because it is continually supporting organizational needs and priorities. As the organization changes direction, leadership, and priorities, the PMO must adjust accordingly. Establish a model that allows for the opportunity to learn from the past to prepare for the future. This is how PMOs exhibit ongoing value to the organization.

When you establish a project management office, be willing to fight for the CAUSE. The CAUSE contains five fundamental components, which we'll explore in detail in later chapters. These are:

- **C**ommunicate
- **A**dvocate
- **U**nderstand
- **S**ystemize
- **E**ffect

As you design the plan to implement a project management office, keep targets clear and distinct. Focus on project management disciplines first. Once the organization gains a proficiency in project management practice and experiences real results, you can modify the plan so the tools, techniques, and discipline applied to project management can be adjusted to address other areas of organizational concern.

Factors in a Successful Launch

A successful PMO launch requires top-down leadership, cross-organizational understanding, clear and constant communication, and an understanding that everyone learns in different ways at their own pace.

When preparing for the launch, develop a project management concept package. This is a promotional kit that can be presented to various departments and at all levels in the organization. The package should include the following elements:

- Basic project management approach and tool kit
- Clear articulation of the problems the approach will solve, why it is different, and the next steps
- Clear expectations of executives, operating unit leaders, project leaders, project managers and the central Project Management Office
- Target "go live" dates

When selling the package to executives, spend lots of time with the executive sponsor who is endorsing the creation of a PMO. Schedule frequent meetings to provide activity updates and ultimately receive approval of the approach. Regular briefings to executive staff are important, so that each executive hears the same presentation. Individual sessions with executives are also important; one-on-one meetings with business leaders are necessary to identify key contacts in their areas, pinpoint key projects, and hear their concerns and ideas.

Gaining operational support is necessary, as establishing a project management methodology cannot occur without their involvement and endorsement. Introduce the new project management approach at departmental staff meetings. Offer follow-up meetings with each operating unit that is critical to the successful launch of the new methodology. At follow-up meetings, identify important process steps unique to each unit, such as length of time for regulatory approval, mandated publications, customer requirements, or a critical process associated with each unit.

Introducing a new EPMO unit warrants some fanfare. Public endorsement of the new approach should be made by the most senior executive, ideally the CEO or COO. This senior leader should further promote his or her understanding by providing an overview of the new approach to staff. EPMO staff should be introduced to the organization and should be available to address questions.

Dedicated Space

When establishing an EPMO, deliberately carve out dedicated space for the unit. Allocating space for the PMO function further endorses the existence of the EPMO and legitimizes its existence to the rest of the organization. Space should include a combination of meeting room space and cubicles/office space for EPMO staff. Regardless of EPMO size, the combination of workspace and meeting space is crucial; one without the other will not provide full-service PMO capability. Dedicated space creates a community of project management activities, which generates energy. A well-defined project management "neighborhood" sends a loud message to the organization in a formal and supportive voice. A PMO community establishes a physical presence and is known for the place in which "stuff happens"; having a secure address on the corporate map reinforces corporate commitment to the EPMO's existence.

Dedicated meeting room space is quite important, because it acts as a "hub" for the organization. Many important events and activities occur in central PMO meeting space—project planning meetings, risk mitigation activities for projects in trouble, and education sessions. A busy meeting schedule represents acceptance of an EPMO and exhibits acknowledgement of the PMO's value to the organization. Consider the environment of the meeting space; create a room with lots of whiteboard space, easels, and markers. Snacks, drinks, and stress-relieving gadgets create a welcoming, supportive atmosphere, and an environment conducive to producing results.

Set the Pace

Setting the right pace while supporting the business plan is as important as the plan itself. For organizations, regardless of current business condition, finding the right pace can be difficult, as many organizations either propel themselves out of the gate too quickly or cannot get themselves out of the gate at all. Launching project management activities before project management processes are set will create re-work and confusion, adding to the exhaustion factor. Alternately, taking too much time to ensure all project management processes are in place before doing the work will cause significant delays in executing the business plan.

A newly organized PMO has the double challenge of getting the organization on board while recognizing that everyone learns in different ways at his or her own pace. Introducing new project management methodology and tools is tricky; the PMO is burdened with gaining corporate endorsement of new project management practices while under pressure to produce measurable results. Finding the right pace for any organization is often done through trial and error. For example, if you tiptoe across the organization while trying to launch project management methodology, you will maintain low awareness of project management among staff. This will result in low compliance with project management practices, and a lack of hitting true deadlines.

During Harvard Pilgrim's time of crisis, HPHC did not have an organized set of processes to support business planning activities. There was no time to plan; survival required immediate action. Tactical execution of the plan, at that time, was done at high velocity, with little time for pause. During this time, the PMO prescribed a rhythmic pace for the organization through meeting facilitation and oversight of action items in a well-choreographed manner. The PMO enforced accountability by monitoring the progress of issue owners and assigned due dates.

Setting the right pace for an organization in crisis is critical; there is a dire need to get out of the gate quickly, but not so quickly that the company exhausts itself before reaching the finish line. Establishing the right pace is equally important for stable organizations attempting to establish a PMO; the PMO must have the ability to set a proper pace for the organization, so people do not give up before they see results. Finding the right pace for a stable organization is often more difficult, as successful businesses are often too lethargic in executing the business plan. If there is no looming disaster, organizations often misjudge the need to be efficient in delivering the work.

How HPHC Handled Pace

HPHC's crisis forced a sense of urgency and discipline that cannot be replicated, particularly now that the crisis is over. The past state of turmoil created a burning platform for HPHC; not having the time to think about process actually allowed the organization to focus only on what was absolutely necessary for survival. Oddly enough, once this crisis phase passed, some things became more difficult. No longer driven by urgency, the burning platform cooled. HPHC faced a new challenge: how to maintain focus in the absence of urgency.

HPHC's turnaround and subsequent successes required the organization to establish new processes to remain focused on priorities and to sustain the discipline required to remain results-oriented. HPHC had established a few project management processes and the results were evident. After seeing tangible results in 1999 and 2000, HPHC took their foot off the gas in 2001 and 2002, and amazingly enough, the executives said, "We're losing our focus, we're falling behind, we're not getting the stuff done the way we used to." The executives basically asked the CEO and COO to re-institute the EPMO. Tough medicine, but they knew they needed it. By 2003, HPHC needed to think about its future and set the strategic direction for the next few years. The strategic plan needed to be nourished with more project management fundamentals in order to flourish. We'll explore the first of these fundamentals, strategic portfolio management, in Chapter 2.

Chapter 2

Strategic Portfolio Management

Being busy does not always mean real work. The object of all work is production or accomplishment and to either of these ends there must be forethought, system, planning, intelligence, and honest purpose, as well as perspiration. Seeming to do is not doing.

Thomas A. Edison

You Can't Manage the Plan Until You Create The Plan

In an environment of increasing demands and stagnant resources, businesses must be precise in evaluating their priorities and setting the "right" agenda. Choosing the right set of projects that properly align to business goals and optimizing limited resources to support the project portfolio are enormous challenges for most organizations. Over the past few years, businesses have begun to realize that selecting the "right" projects is key to realizing organizational and business strategy. The process and rationale by which project decisions get made will vary from organization to organization. Much of this variation is due to the high level of subjectiveness embedded in the process. The key to an efficient portfolio development process is establishing the right balance between clear criteria for prioritization and selection on the one hand, and the need for simplicity and results on the other.

During Harvard Pilgrim's time of crisis, HPHC did not have an organized set of processes to support business-planning activities. There was no time to plan; survival required immediate action. In fact, the "business plan" in 1999 included a 150-day effort to recalibrate the organization for survival. Senior leaders met weekly to

18

develop, chart, and monitor strategy, tactics, and actions related to the turnaround plan. And they did it at a frenzied pace. The Project Management Office (PMO) supported those activities through meeting facilitation and issue tracking. They enforced accountability by tracking issue owners and due dates. In many instances, the PMO acted as air traffic controllers, providing an organized flight pattern to ensure safe project takeoff and landing for the work activities that were flying in all directions. The PMO tool kit was easel sheets, markers, and Post-It Notes. But the key to the PMO's success at the time was not the tools in the kit; it was their neutral position within the organization and their action-oriented focus. Their ability to support vigor with real results during chaos, coupled with their passion to succeed, aided Harvard Pilgrim's triumphant turnaround.

Once it reached stability, HPHC needed to do what other organizations are challenged with: think about the future and set the strategic direction for the next few years. What is the PMO's role in supporting this objective? It is to facilitate the process through which the organization can effectively make the right choices about which projects will most significantly influence its future.

The PMO's primary role is to assume a neutral position and guide the enterprise through the project selection process. The PMO can administer the process, facilitate the identification of selection criteria, and maintain a clear audit trail of how decisions are made. To be effective in this role, the PMO must extend its purview beyond pure project management practice and become more strategic in aligning the portfolio selection process with corporate needs. The PMO must also remain strong in its position to never be the decision-maker. Making the decisions about which projects will offer the best return for the organization's future falls to senior executives. The members of the executive team who are responsible for setting the corporate strategic direction should also be the ones to make the decision about corporate priority initiatives.

Once the turnaround was underway at HPHC, the next act required the company to reflect on the past to anticipate the future and depend on reliable business processes to establish a model for creating a future-facing, strategic direction. Keeping a constant focus on the organization's future and creating easy, sustainable activities that align with company goals and objectives can help set the direction and maintain the pace. Again, it is a simple model that requires only minimal oversight and administration.

A good business plan demands set principles, reliable processes, and measurable targets. Business planning is usually preceded by review and determination of a strategic direction, a set of corporate goals, and key performance metrics for the upcoming year. This chapter does not suggest strategic planning processes. Instead, it focuses on what to do once the strategic direction is set. To succeed, organizations must have well-defined processes in place to smoothly transition from strategic vision to portfolio building. Having a process that guides the organization from strategic vision to tactical planning is key; a company cannot manage the plan until the critical building blocks are identified. Projects are the critical building blocks in achieving an organization's strategic plan.

Since the PMO does not lead strategic planning activities, there is typically an alliance between the Strategic Development Department and the PMO to ensure a smooth transition. Strategic Development is responsible for driving the major components in support of strategic plan development. The PMO is accountable for supporting the process through facilitative, analytical, and supportive activities, and for guiding the organization through tactical planning. At HPHC, such an alliance exists. Members of the Strategic Development department and the enterprise-level PMO (EPMO) meet on a weekly basis to assess the current portfolio, to discuss any new projects on the horizon, and gauge the temperature of issues that impact successful and timely business plan delivery.

David Cochran, M.D., Senior Vice President, Strategic Development at HPHC, strongly believes members of both areas should meet on a regular basis to assess the current state of the portfolio. The meetings allow each side of the equation—planning and execution—to balance each other to ensure successful business plan realization. Why is this important? According to Dr. Cochran, it is necessary because "success is dependent on setting a direction, making reasonable commitments, and delivering." The two areas must partner throughout the year, not just during business planning activities. Cochran adds, "It's critical that the strategic direction and business commitments be informed by the capabilities of the enterprise and that the strategic priorities be reflected in the tradeoffs that have to be made in delivering the portfolio."

The portfolio never stays static; it often changes due to shifts in environment, legislation, and business need. Because of the constant motion, frequent sessions between the two departments are required to ensure the organization remains focused on the priority targets and that resources are appropriately assigned. "Close collaboration between Strategic Planning and Project Management functions has made this interplay vibrant and successful at HPHC," says Cochran.

The PMO must have some fundamental capabilities in place to guide the portfolio process. The elements include:

- A process for prioritization and selection,
- An understanding of budget and resource capacity,
- Commitment to use the process,
- Ability to measure portfolio success, and
- Willingness to improve the process based upon stakeholder feedback.

One of the biggest challenges is defining a process for project prioritization and selection. The process cannot be cumbersome, as too many review gates will slow down the approval process. At the same time, an organization needs clear criteria for prioritization and selection so the system cannot be manipulated. Establish simple criteria that define the attributes a project must have to be considered for inclusion. The criteria must set guidelines for how a project aligns with the strategic plan.

At HPHC, a Business Oversight Committee is responsible for developing multi-year business plans and budgets to achieve the corporate goals. This committee also monitors the process of developing the corporate business plan and operating budgets. The committee consists of a cross-functional team of senior executives, who develop and recommend annual and multi-year business plans for discussion and approval by HPHC's Executive Committee. Once the plans and budgets are approved, the Oversight Committee is also responsible for monitoring the plan's effectiveness. Leveraging corporate processes, the Strategic Development Department, the Business Oversight Committee, and the PMO come together to ensure the business plan is developed according to schedule and delivered according to scope and deadline. It requires collaboration, flexibility, and mutual respect for individual roles and responsibilities across the group to orchestrate the business plan in a unified and timely fashion.

Selecting the "Right" Portfolio

HPHC's portfolio development process consists of three phases: Nomination, Prioritization, and Selection. The process is uncomplicated, so the activities are easy, repeatable, and reliable. Keeping the process simple promotes stakeholder buy-in and does not require a tremendous investment of time. When you ask senior executives to participate in a set of activities, it is critical to keep the procedure undemanding. Introducing a straightforward process that requires minimal time and produces clear results will guarantee executive endorsement and a high level of engagement.

The three-phase process is a valid way for senior executives to present business cases consistently, so all cases can be evaluated equitably and selected appropriately. Without guidelines in place, the project proposed by the most charismatic executive is more likely to be approved for portfolio inclusion. Having standard criteria in place helps level the playing field. Project presentations are made with one goal in mind: to show how they contribute to the organization's goals and generate value.

Phase One: Nomination

The nomination phase is a standard, concise way for business leaders to nominate initiatives that best support the organization's corporate goals. A standard presentation template is used for all nominations. Business leaders are asked to present their nominations in no more than 10 or 15 minutes, and must address the following areas: Business Opportunity, Project Goal, Expected Business Outcomes, Risks if

Project is Not Done, Project Interdependencies, and Risks to Project Success.

As we examine each area individually, we'll also look at our case study, "Vendor Fulfillment Change," through the Nomination lens.

Business Opportunity:
This defines the particular business opportunity or problem the project addresses. Also known as the "problem statement," this is the first chance to state the problem the organization is trying to solve, in a form that is factual and true to the entire organization.

Case Study Problem Statement:
"The current vendor does not meet HPHC expectation. Eight major initiatives with current vendor this year were late, jeopardizing business and cost objectives. Over 68% of all current vendor management reports have errors and result in an inability to tie weekly reports to actual production. Only 20% of invoices are received on time or in correct format, resulting in difficult and time-consuming invoice reconciliation. HPHC has the opportunity to replace its current fulfillment vendor with vendor partner(s) that will provide the following benefits:

- Improve overall vendor fulfillment customer service (e.g., problem-solving production issues)
- Reduce fulfillment cost by eliminating identification card stock and implementing print-on-demand technology
- Reduce the administrative complexity of the day-to-day management of invoicing, inventory and quality issues
- Eliminate "exception processing" of kits as a result of current vendor(s) ability to meet all fulfillment requirements.

Project Goal:
The goal concisely summarizes what will be delivered by the project that addresses the business opportunity statement. Ideally, there should be only one goal per project, which is associated with a concrete objective.

Case Study Project Goal:
Select, contract, and implement with new fulfillment vendors. Bring on line with minimal business disruption.

Corporate Goal Alignment:
The project must relate to one of the corporate goals, and ideally support only one goal. In some instances, it is appropriate for a project to support more than one corporate goal. Be careful: alignment with more than one corporate goal does not necessarily give more weight to a nomination. Stress the need to correlate the project alignment with one key corporate goal, to keep the process clean and fair.

Case Study Corporate Goal Alignment:
Meet or exceed our financial targets.

Expected Business Outcome(s):
The nomination should include quantifiable measures of success beyond the standard success definition (which revolves around scope, schedule and budget). Include explicit measures for business outcomes, avoiding such words as "significantly," "acceptable," or "attempt." Instead, the measures should include time, numbers, and percentages.

Case Study Expected Business Outcomes:

Description: Cost reduction through print-on-demand implementation and new contract
Current Metric: N/A
Expected Metric: Reduction of $65,000 committed in 2005 budget, by reducing card stock to one (1)

Description: Contract savings (2005 budget)
Current Metric: N/A
Expected Metric: $90,000 committed

Description: Eliminate physical inventory management
Current Metric: On-hand inventory 181,000 kit items
Expected Metric: No preprinted items; Adobe files printed on demand in a pdf booklet (shell)
Description: Vendor Service Level Agreement in place; No internal fulfillment metrics
Current Metric: Vendor reports monthly metrics:
  TAT Cards: 99.92% (24 hrs)
  TAT kits: 85% (48 hrs)
  TAT EOBs, EOPs Invoices, Pends: 100% (48 hrs)
  Production Standards: Not available today
Expected Metric: TAT Cards: 99.92% (24 hrs)
  TAT kits: 99.9% (48 hrs)
  TAT EOBs, EOPs Invoices, Pends: 100% (48 hrs)
  SLA will be in place
  Production Standards: To be developed

Risks if Project is Not Done:
Executives can present this information in a variety of ways, through either precise measurement or predictive modeling. A typical opening comment may sound like this: "If this project is not done, the company will experience X …"

Case Study Risks:
If this project is not done, the company will experience continued escalating administrative costs and member dissatisfaction.

Project Interdependencies:
It is important to understand whether the nomination relies on another project or another project relies upon the nominated project to succeed. It's like playing a game of dominoes—you can't remove one tile without impacting another.

Case Study Interdependencies:
The project identified interdependent relationships with four other priority initiatives.

Risks to Project Success:
This is a high-level risk assessment. A simple High-Medium-Low scale is a useful tool for doing this.

High: Organization has no experience with this type of project, so there's a high opportunity for risks to occur.

Medium: Some experience with this type of project, medium opportunity for risks to occur.

Low: High experience with this type of project, unlikely opportunity for risks occurring.

Estimated Resource Draw:
The work effort should not determine the initiative's level of importance to the business plan, but it is helpful to understand how long the initiative may last and what level of resources it will use. A simple High-Medium-Low scale is all that is needed at this point in time.

High: More than 15 FTE's
Medium: 7 to 15 FTE's
Low: 1 to 6 FTE's

Case Study Risk Level:
This project was identified as having a Medium level of risk.

Assessing the information associated with work effort is tricky, and understanding the level of work effort associated with a project does not necessarily dictate priority. However, knowing if you have the organizational capacity to deliver on your priorities is important.

Executive sponsors of each project make all nominations. Requiring senior executives to present the information holds each of them accountable for knowing the content of the project, being able to articulate why the project is important, and recognizing the level of effort associated with the project. It is too easy for executive sponsors to sidestep this responsibility by delegating the presentation to a project manager. This requirement also insists senior executives effectively translate project benefits into the language of corporate goals. This forces both the presenter and the audience to hear presentations in a uniform manner, all focused on organizational success.

The PMO plays an important role in the nomination process by creating the standard nomination template and informing executives about what is required by when. The PMO also coordinates the nomination information in a sequenced and comprehensive package. Even though HPHC's PMO offers continuous training and outreach on how to best present project nominations, the PMO often finds itself offering guidance and suggestions to those responsible for producing project nominations, to ensure their business cases contain all key elements presented in a uniform manner.

During the Nomination phase, audience members consider a few guiding questions to help them assimilate the information and prepare themselves for the next phase. Here are some questions they may consider while listening to nominations:

- Is this project a "must do" (e.g., a mandate)?
- Will this work help the organization gain a strategic advantage?
- Does this work directly support our growth objectives?
- Does this work directly support our financial goals?
- Can efforts be made to narrow the scope of the project so we only do the necessary and the critical?

The Nomination phase can be streamlined through standardized presentation templates and a commitment to keeping nomination presentations within a set time limit. It is necessary and expected for the presenter to know the project information. Allow time for questions and answers, as it is equally important for the other committee members to also understand the nominations. A global understanding of all nominations is essential before moving on to the Prioritization phase.

Phase Two: Prioritization

Once all nominations have been heard, the Prioritization phase begins. This phase forces business operations committee members to review the nominations and consider each of the initiatives with respect to one another. Your organization must establish prioritization criteria before the process begins. The qualities a project must have in order to proceed can include strategic alignment, risk, resource availability, level of work effort, and interdependent relationships. While the criteria are important, having everyone understand them and be able to consistently evaluate projects using the criteria is more important. HPHC applies a system that generates quantitative values based on subjective judgments. (The practice was adopted from *Project Portfolio Management: Selecting and Prioritizing Projects for Competitive Advantage* by Lowell D. Dye and James S. Pennypacker.)

This system includes an exercise also known as the Poor Man's Hierarchy, and is intended to enable decision-makers to rank order portfolio options in a relatively painless fashion. After identifying prioritization criteria, decision-makers compare each nomination pairwise. HPHC executives find this exercise difficult because it requires participants to remember each of the nominations, recall the salient points of each presentation, and then, while considering each project, determine which is more important. Here is an example of the Pairwise Grid.

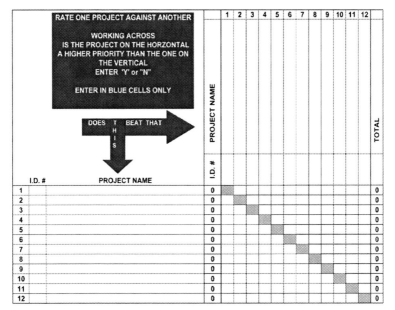

Figure 2-1—Pairwise Grid

Here's how the exercise works. Cells in the grid are filled in accord-ing to the following rule: If the initiative along the side of the grid is preferable to the initiative listed across the top, then a "Y" is placed in the cell. If the initiative on the top is preferred, place an "N" in the cell. Note that the gray diagonal cells are blanked out, since it does not make sense to compare a project to itself.

The outcome of this exercise provides input into how each deci-sion-maker sees the relative importance of initiatives. The collective results show where there is agreement on priorities and where there are significant differences among perspectives that the group should discuss. The Pairwise exercise is only a guide for determining portfolio priorities; the exercise does not provide conclusive results, nor does it adequately confirm the relative sequence of priorities—business is seldom that precise. What it *does* do is provide a basis for correlative discussion, which supports the overall prioritization process.

Deborah Norton is a member of HPHC's Business Oversight Committee and has participated in pairwise activities. Describing the exercise as "comparing apples and oranges," Norton terms the exercise difficult because, "Sometimes the resources needed to support one project are very different than those needed to support another, yet the user is asked to force rank initiatives that on the surface appear to have no relationship to one another. This creates a certain sense of frustration and anxiety."

Despite this, Norton believes the process works. "The user must confront what is most important, e.g., regulatory compliance versus new product development. And the less important, lower-priority items drop from the list, allowing the user to focus on what's most important." Norton's experience suggests the structured discipline of force ranking surfaces the sometimes implicit bias of the business and forces the question about priorities. "So, while frustrating, the structure of the process brings order to the chaos of new ideas and 'must do's.'"

In addition to the Pairwise exercise, the PMO provides additional sets of data and information, ranging from a Dependency Map (shows which projects directly depend on another project in order to succeed) to a Portfolio Balancing Map (illustrates the number of projects associated with each corporate goal). This is a great way to determine if you have a proper balance of initiatives in support of the overall business plan.

Phase Three: Selection

Once a prioritized list of projects emerges, the group inspects the list again to understand how resources (human and capital) impact operations and other critical activities within each functional area. Participants review the list of projects against several constraints, including capital requirements and resource availability. The goal of this session is to identify the risks and tradeoffs among the projects on the list, balanced against "lights-on" work (existing work), and to identify the major resource gaps.

Since organizations seldom have the capacity to do every project nominated, this exercise forces executive sponsors to consider options for their project nominations. For example, HPHC will often find instances when a project can be scaled back in scope, requiring fewer resources to support the work, yet still be capable of meeting the business need. Or it may see a way to bundle like projects, leveraging a limited set of subject matter experts. This exercise results in a list of mutually agreed upon, consensus-driven priority initiatives, all of which directly support corporate goals and are likely to be supported by adequate resources.

Assessing resource requirements at this point in the process is the most challenging aspect of the exercise. Even though projects are not yet fully scoped and planning has not yet occurred to project the true resource demand, executives must decide what makes the portfolio list. The PMO can add extraordinary value to this challenge by guiding business leaders through a risk-identification process, using tools and techniques specifically designed to assess how a project will draw on resources. Assessing resource capacity is an onerous task, as many organizations do not have the right tools in place to effectively track how much effort is required to support the work. Even with the right tools in place, however, plenty of organizations do not take the time to develop interventions or contingency plans to support the necessary work—even when the resource draw is apparent. This becomes particularly difficult when assessing project resource draw relative to operations demand.

The whole process of moving from Nomination through Selection typically takes multiple sessions over a two-month period. While this may seem long to some, HPHC has found that the process itself is quite streamlined; the duration from start to finish represents the planned time allowed to support healthy discussion and debate. No matter how precise the data, the systems, or the processes, these major decisions require an engaging exchange of opinions and positions, and an augmentation of objectives.

The PMO plays an integral role in supporting the portfolio development process. It gathers necessary information, instructs participants on tasks, and facilitates the process from start to finish according to corporate deadlines. Because the PMO does not "own" any projects and does not have a vested interest in one project being nominated over another, the PMO is the most valuable player in the process. It provides neutrality while facilitating a business-critical function for the organization as a whole.

Once the portfolio is set, the PMO assumes the role of facilitator, ensuring the organization delivers on the plan. The PMO can direct traffic and unsnarl congestion along the route between strategic vision and project execution.

Balancing the Portfolio

In an ideal world, the list of projects identified during portfolio development remains the same list of projects throughout the year. Unfortunately, business is not that clean. The list of priority projects is subject to change almost as quickly as it is created. This does not suggest the process to build the portfolio is flawed; it does, however, highlight the challenges involved in maintaining strong strategic direction amidst changing business conditions.

Initiatives initially identified as priorities are typically the ones selected at the beginning of a business planning cycle, which is a particular point in time—a snapshot. However, business is dynamic; organizations must be able to respond to new opportunities and challenges that arise or were originally unforeseen. An organization must be able to remain competitive and viable, which depends upon its ability to be agile. In some instances, this means being able to add to a list of priorities during the year and then reallocating resources to support them. Since organizations have limited resources (both capital and human) to support projects, they cannot simply keep adding items to the portfolio.

Effective portfolio balancing must occur to ensure all senior leaders agree on what is important (the items to remain on the list), what changes need to occur (what gets added to the list), and what trade-offs must be made (what comes off the list or gets delayed).

At HPHC, the process for balancing the portfolio is similar to the one used for building the portfolio. All new project requests must be presented as a new Nomination, using the standard Nomination template. New projects are assessed against existing ones in terms of corporate goal alignment, dependency relationships, and implementation requirements. In other words, new nominations are evaluated against the existing portfolio to assess them in terms of business priority and organizational ability to support the work.

The balancing process can and should be an abbreviated version of the portfolio building process; using the Nomination, Prioritization and Selection process works well in both situations. In other words, keep the process simple to be effective. The key ingredient for keeping both the portfolio building and the portfolio balancing processes successful is communication, which we will explore in Chapter 3.

CHAPTER 3

COMMUNICATE

Think like a wise man but communicate in the language of the people.

William Butler Yeats

Communicating the Vision

The real power of a corporate vision is realized only when everyone in the organization clearly understands the vision and recognizes how everyone contributes to its success. Easier said than done. In most organizations, only a handful of people really understand the mission and how it translates to corporate objectives, and how the objectives realize priority projects.

It is equally important for everyone to know how the company is delivering on the priorities. Project managers tend to see only their own projects, and they are unsure how the project they are managing supports the organization's overall success. Many project sponsors don't take the time to understand the status of project activities and are often unable to recognize the early warning signs of a project in trouble. Senior executives seldom conduct a check-in on the business plan as a whole to ask questions like these: Is it still the right plan? Does it require adjustment? Do we need to shuffle priorities? Are we properly resourced to deliver the priorities? And most staffers on the front lines do not really understand how their day-to-day efforts support the mission.

The PMO plays a key role in connecting the dots and communicating key headlines throughout the organization so there is a global understanding of, and commitment to, the successful delivery of the business plan. The traditional PMO typically focuses on communicating individual project activities, only *after* projects have launched. It is right for the PMO to focus on project communications, as this is the hub of their existence. However, the PMO also has a responsibility to communicate the portfolio as it is being developed and while it is being executed; sharing this information across the enterprise enables a heightened level of understanding, which further promotes plan success.

Once project status communications have been established, the PMO should expand the communication methods, tools, and practices to extend beyond projects, so all stakeholders in the organization—regardless of position and role—understand what is important to the organization and recognize how they contribute to the business plan's success. The PMO is the most logical facilitator of this effort, as it has the most intimate knowledge of business plan details. However, the PMO must collaborate with others across the enterprise to produce a meaningful communications plan.

Business Plan Communications

At HPHC, the PMO partners with the marketing and strategic development departments to design and deploy a well-orchestrated internal communications plan that tells employees about the business plan. The purpose of the communications plan is to provide employees with a line of sight from the company's brand, mission, values, goals and performance to their day-to-day work. The communications plan helps staff understand the overarching business strategy, the priorities (and why), the tradeoffs the organization needs to make short-term and long-term, and what to expect (and what is expected of them) each year. The plan must be straightforward and comprehensible to effectively inform all staff. The idea is to create simple messages, and be creative about making the messages memorable. Then you must repeat. Repeat. Repeat. HPHC finds that creating some of the corporate plan communications in a conversational and interactive format allows employees to relate to the information better. HPHC has accomplished this through the use of Q&A's and manager tool kits (more on these later).

Before creating your communications plan, meet with the executives who have the greatest number of employees affected by the corporate agenda so you can fully understand the employee impacts and concerns/fears/aspirations of staff. Doing this is important because it helps you to frame the communication in a way that is relevant and meaningful to staff. Conduct informal focus groups among business leaders and staff to hear from them, in their own words, what they need to know and why. The process for collecting this input does not need to be long, but it is an important one. Some of the questions to consider when interviewing business leaders include:

- What is top-of-mind for your employees today?
- What do your employees know about the corporate agenda?
- Do you think our current value proposition provides the right/ helpful strategic context for the current corporate agenda? If not, what is missing?
- What are the three most critical messages we need to communicate to employees around the current corporate agenda?
- Any thoughts on how best to communicate these messages?

Using previous communications plans as your guide, consider the following questions for staff:

- Did you understand last year's business plan and were you able to recognize how your work contributes to its success?
- Were previous communication channels effective? How can we improve them?
- Did we sequence communications in a way that made sense and were the communications released in a timely fashion?
- Was your management team well-informed about the corporate agenda and were they able to respond to your questions?

Feedback from executives and staff allows you to stay focused on the basic intent of the communications plan. This input will allow you to improve each year and maintain a high level of engagement among staff.

Manager Tool Kits

At HPHC, manager tool kits are designed to provide key messages managers can use when communicating business plan information to staff. Print and electronic communications build employee awareness, but to reach true understanding and engagement, managers must have two-way conversations with their employees about the business plan. The tool kit, developed by the Strategic Internal Communications Department, provides the manager with talking points, a scripted PowerPoint presentation, and tips for customizing content and delivery. A Q&A tool that assists management with typical anticipated questions is also included in the kit. The tool kit provides management with important information that can be delivered across the organization in a consistent fashion, irrespective of who delivers it. It ensures key business units will hear the same information, regardless of where they sit in the organization. It also is written in a way that strengthens key messages, reinforcing what is important for the organization's future success and why certain work efforts are considered priorities.

In addition to standard business plan information, manager tool kits also include customized content, which provides further business plan context and outlines the role employees play within specific business units. This allows individual business units to identify the project(s) that their unit will lead and those in which they will play a substantial supporting role. With key initiatives identified, managers can provide more detail by sharing two or three key tasks relative to the project, and can express department expectations about fulfilling project requirements. Individual business units can also identify day-to-day business operations activities that will still need to be taken care of while the unit supports project requirements.

In some instances, business units are forced to identify tradeoffs—activities they will need to forego to get the priority work done. Stating the requirements up front diminishes confusion later and allows managers to clearly state performance expectations to staff. This forum also enables managers to inform employees where they should go if they have specific questions or concerns relative to any of the information presented.

Providing consistent messaging and content to the managers who deliver the information across the organization is important; reminding managers how to best deliver the information is also necessary. While every manager has a unique communication style, it is sometimes in the company's best interest to remind managers how to convey key messages most effectively. Include guidelines in the tool kit to assist managers with information delivery—simple guidelines are most effective. Here are a few suggestions:

- Consider how to best cascade information throughout your particular business unit.

- Deliver information face-to-face to allow for two-way communication.

- Prepare questions to ask employees; this gauges the employees' understanding.

- Answering with "I don't know" is okay; follow-up is key.

Design a Multi-Channel Approach

Design a multi-channel approach to inform staff about what is critical for the organization's future success, explain how the organization will deliver the work, and provide ongoing progress reports. Leverage different mediums and create multiple forums to deliver the message. This allows you to effectively reach all staff across the organization on an ongoing basis and to celebrate success stories as they happen throughout the year.

Mary Ellen Conlon, Manager, Strategic Internal Communications Department at HPHC, believes messages are most effective when all the communication channels are working together. She uses a multi-channel approach to reach all employees. "I envision employees reading about the business plan in the corporate newsletter, accessing information from the company's Intranet, listening to the CEO at 'Town Meetings' and discussing the plan with their managers at weekly staff meetings." Mary Ellen uses this vision to create the comprehensive plan.

Today, it is easier than ever to offer information through multiple channels. Recognize that everyone processes information differently.

When you understand audience differences, you can create a series of messages that contain different levels of information and deliver it through a variety of channels. In addition to manager tool kits, HPHC offers business plan information through slide shows, audio voice-overs, posters, weekly newsletters via email, and CEO memos. The options are endless—understand what your organization needs, how staff best respond to receiving the information, and then create a plan that supports business plan activities throughout the year.

The Event

Harvard Pilgrim's PMO produces an all-staff event each year to educate, engage, and energize staff regarding the corporate business plan. The half-day event takes a plenary/trade show format that lets staff learn about the priority initiatives, the operating departments, and overall collaborative efforts.

The annual event follows a standard program for presenting information, yet each year the event somehow adds variety to the way information is shared. Previous events have included staff-performed skits, which told stories that resonated with HPHC's business plan and explained why the work was important. HPHC also invites keynote speakers who address HPHC staff on a business concept that aligns with the corporate business plan and correlates to Harvard Pilgrim's future success.

Trade show booths introduce corporate projects to employees by describing the initiative, explaining how it fits into the overall plan, and why it is important. Business units are also invited to spotlight themselves through a booth exhibit. This is a fun and informative way to enhance staff's understanding of HPHC's different business units. It also improves staff's ability to support and promote intra- and interdepartmental teamwork. It is a terrific way to get all staff together in one location, have face-to-face interaction with senior executives, and encounter colleagues they deal with on a regular basis, yet seldom have the chance to meet. Not only do people leave more informed about HPHC's priorities, they also feel a sense of pride in having the opportunity to put their work in the spotlight. It is a great way to build a sense of spirit and collaboration. This is a perfect example of where the PMO has enhanced value to the organization, by looking outside the traditional project management box.

Campaigns

A great way to establish a sense of urgency around the priority work and to produce a way to celebrate small wins is the use of campaigns. Campaigns come in a variety of models; HPHC designs campaign efforts similar to political campaigns—to win the hearts and minds of staff. Campaigns are an easy way to execute your vision by consolidating the organization's efforts into a theme and then communicating the victories. Start the campaign as soon as work is announced and establish the duration of the campaign. Clearly identify each objective of the campaign and be sure to announce each accomplishment as it occurs.

HPHC's experience suggests all such campaigns are won because of three factors:

1. The power of the message: Establish a message that resonates with all staff. Make it a simple message that is easy to remember and too powerful to forget. Use visuals or logos to promote the message. Place campaign posters in common areas, where staff will see them on a regular basis.

2. The strength and ability of the people: Your staff is great! Acknowledge the power of people's past accomplishments to rely on their ability to rally around the campaign's goal. Announce victories as soon as they are won; visually track the accomplishments.

3. The strength of the logistics, support and planning: Think of the EPMO as the "campaign management office." Use proven tools to plan, organize, and communicate the campaign.

A few years back, HPHC ran a very effective campaign to rally staff around the final thirteen weeks of completing key deliverables for successfully meeting a corporate goal. It was appropriately named "Baker's Dozen," and focused attention on efforts to achieve a profitable year. HPHC played off the name to rally staff around important activities that needed to occur to meet key objectives. It was an easy way for staff to remember the number thirteen; it also referenced "Baker," the name of HPHC's CEO. Updates on corporate efforts and achievements were issued in a weekly all-staff newsletter. Campaign posters were placed in public areas and were updated weekly to include key achievements.

As milestones for each project were reached, mini-celebrations were staged in company cafeterias, where cookies were served to staff as a token of appreciation for their efforts and in recognition of the company's success. Over 2,000 cookies were offered at "Baker's Dozen" displays at office locations. HPHC knows staff paid attention to the cookies, and believes everyone took the time to see what they accomplished during the 13-week period. This is an example of how a relatively small effort in support of organizational efforts during complex times can be easy, yet memorable. The PMO can administer this program through its tracking of key milestones for priority initiatives. Employing simple project management activities and measures supports the campaign process.

Currently, HPHC employs "Stay Ahead of the Curve" as the overarching theme for their 2007 business plan. Conlon, who was a major force in designing the campaign, believes there is a secret to campaign success: "Find a message that will not only resonate with staff, but will mobilize them to take action."

Forums

Forums create an opportunity to inform and educate a general, "live" audience. Intended for smaller audiences, forums are a good way to position and promote activities or subjects that in some way support an organizational business plan. Forum topics can be focused on a theme or key aspect of a business plan. Forums are a great way to inform key staff about priority projects; educate staff on impending legislative issues that may impact the organization's future, or offer educational opportunities with an industry-specific focus. Session timing and length can be adapted to meet desired communications objectives.

At HPHC, the EPMO establishes a forum lineup through outreach to prospective presenters; speakers are promoted through internal communications and posters. Forum audiences have the ability to hear important information in an intimate setting, which allows for a Q&A segment. Most forums at HPHC are held during the lunch hour, to allow all levels of staff to attend.

Staff Newsletters

Many organizations use newsletters for communication. They are popular because they provide important headlines to staff in an easy, predictable way. Newsletters are quick to produce and provide a forum for sharing key information in a simple fashion. The popularity of newsletters has created an interesting challenge for many larger companies—because they work, they tend to be used across many business units throughout an organization. Before you know it, there are many newsletters floating across business units, all sharing "important" messages.

Be careful; too many newsletters carrying too many messages can cause confusion. Companies can successfully manage multiple newsletters if each newsletter serves a primary purpose. For example, there should be only one corporate newsletter, created for the organization as a whole. This publication should be the only publication to communicate key information about corporate activities, including business plan updates. Other newsletters should focus on "local news" only, so not to confuse or dilute key messages.

Portfolio Reporting

Portfolio reporting is the most common method of informing organizations about the progress of project activities. Similar to creating the corporate communications plan, the portfolio report should be designed with multiple audience needs in mind. Since different business stakeholders require different levels of detail associated with project plan activities, it is critical to create a report that is flexible enough to meet everyone's needs. It is equally important to create a reporting mechanism that is easy to produce and conveys the least amount of information necessary to communicate key headlines, activities, or risks associated with achieving project/portfolio success. Producing more information than necessary is likely to cause confusion among recipients. Too much information may be viewed as superfluous, and will be cumbersome to manage. Once again, keep the process simple to be successful.

Know your audience's needs before designing a report. If you are introducing reports for the first time, be extra-careful not to overload your audience with unnecessary information. Identify which elements are the most critical for stakeholders to know about and start with straightforward delivery. There is no "right" method of portfolio reporting. It really does depend on organizational need and style. Be careful of elaborate portfolio reporting tools. They may mesmerize with fancy bells and whistles, yet they may be more than your organization needs. Regardless of how long your PMO has existed, be careful not to create a report that contains too much information too soon. Otherwise, your audience will drown in details.

Whether you fully automate your reporting processes (through an enterprise reporting tool) or you manage the information through home-grown tools and manual processes, be certain to create reports that require minimal oversight to produce the minimum information necessary. Also, categorize what type and level of information are required by each audience and compare their needs to PMO needs. Some information is for public consumption, while other components are appropriate for the PMO only.

Priority corporate initiatives typically include a complex and complicated list of large, cross-functional assignments. Harvard Pilgrim typically averages 40 priority initiatives per year, many interdependent upon each other. Keeping the project status reporting process simple allows the PMO and key stakeholders to maintain a good sense of project status without becoming bogged down in the details. At HPHC, the portfolio report is a series of portfolio views, presented to a broad audience as a full package of information. The package includes both summary and detailed information; recipients have the option to review the package in its entirety or view specific details pertinent to their needs. The PMO collects, reviews, and publishes key project headlines, which include active project activities and project risks. The PMO also maintains a system of exception reporting to focus attention on those projects that are off-target and to describe mitigation activities. Through exception reporting, the bulk of the project portfolio proceeds under the charge of its team and the PMO without consuming executive oversight time.

Project Status Reports

Project managers are required to submit weekly project status reports to the PMO. The status report is a simple, standard way of consistently communicating project activities and allows project managers the opportunity to alert project stakeholders to issues impeding project success. It is imperative to have a clear understanding at the start of each project, including knowing the outputs and schedule of the critical deliverables anticipated from each project. Having this baseline sets performance expectations for each initiative.

At HPHC, project managers record project status with the simple "Red-Yellow-Green" system. Each status is clearly defined, yet project stakeholders often need to be reminded of their meaning. The PMO should generate gentle prompts regarding status definitions on a routine basis. Keep the definitions basic, so not to confuse interpretation.

Green = all project activities proceeding according to plan
Yellow = corrective action is being taken
Red = senior management attention is required

Understanding true project status is critically important to the PMO, yet it is not always easy to decipher. In spite of simple definitions and instructions to project managers, it is not always easy to identify true project status or why a project has changed status. One simple request may solve this problem. When a project is Yellow or Red, ask for the reason for the change. HPHC handles this with a simple approach: all summary updates start with: "The project is Yellow/

Red because…" The summary should also include the game plan for getting back on track.

Project managers must understand the importance of accurate status reporting, as the information they publish each week is one of the best ways for a PMO to monitor project activity and to assess project health. Mary Joyce, a project manager at HPHC, explains why accurate status reporting is so important at HPHC.

"Project managers at HPHC must record accurate status on the project status report (PSR), as the Red/Yellow/Green coding is an extremely powerful tool that acts as a 'call to action' for executives. For example, if I submit my project status as Red, my project will be in the 'spotlight' with all the executives in the organization. By moving my status from Yellow to Red, I have sent them a signal that my project is in need of something—a decision, more resources, etc. Through the PMO status reporting process, my project gets the attention it deserves and the focus of the executives to take action to turn my project back to Green. As a Project Manager (PM), you don't want to abuse this tool—you could be known as 'the PM who cried wolf/Red too often,' and future projects you are attached to might not get the attention they deserve to be successful."

Joyce adds: "The ease of determining the 'real' status of your project depends on the complexity of your project and the size of your project team. It is always good to take a commonsense approach when you determine the status of your project before pushing the 'submit' button on your PSR. For my own projects, I use a three status rule. If my project status is Yellow for three reporting periods, I evaluate the movement on the issues that originally turned it from Green to Yellow. If there has been no movement, I move the status to Red. Three reporting periods is a very long time in the life of a project, in my opinion."

This approach depends on creating a business culture that supports early problem identification so issues can be addressed in a timely fashion and "no news" truly *is* "good news." This system is effective only when senior executives publicly support early, honest declaration of project derailment. Project managers will not practice this behavior if they are not supported in their actions. Disclosing early warning signs must be promoted as a positive behavior, because an early signal often allows early intervention—before the situation becomes dire. This is a cultural challenge for many organizations, as most companies maintain the traditional stance of equating public disclosure of derailment with failure, rather than regarding it as a proactive plea for help.

Case Study:
The Vendor Fulfillment project submitted a total of 53 status reports (representing 53 weeks of activity) between October 22, 2004 and November 10, 2005. Over 70% of submitted project status reports indicated a "Yellow" status. The reasons for the Yellow state were varied, yet can be summarized like this:

- Project status remained Yellow during the Planning phase; challenges included delays in securing needed resources and holdups in confirming project schedule.

- Key decisions were required from senior executives during the vendor selection process. Alerting executives to impending deadlines was accomplished through a Yellow flag.

- Reliance on external vendors always adds complexity. This project relied upon multiple vendors, increasing project risks for timely delivery from outside partners.

Portfolio Summary Package

The weekly report includes a portfolio summary page, which lists all active projects, organized according to business goal. It identifies assigned executive sponsors, project leads and project managers for each project, and declares current project status.

A portfolio trend page lists all active projects, project stakeholders, the project end date, and additional summary status details for the current reporting period. It also includes a trend report for the previous three-week period. The trend information is valuable, because it is a good mechanism for tracking project status over a period of time, as well as for indicating project changes.

Executive Project Status Report

Executives have limited time to review project status reports, so it is key to create a report that focuses on important information *only*. At HPHC, weekly project status reports are collected and summarized in an executive project status report, which is distributed to senior executives and other corporate stakeholders. The report focuses on "exceptions" only: Red and Yellow projects that require focused attention and discussion regarding current status and mitigation strategies.

Using the executive report as a guide, the Yellow and Red statuses are reviewed and discussed at senior leadership meetings. HPHC's PMO leader presents the data on behalf of project managers and executive sponsors, and highlights areas of risk in achieving project success (which translate to business plan success). Effective delivery of information requires frequent observation of project activities, conversation with project team members, and an understanding of project dependencies. This regular discussion ensures that senior executives are aware of priority initiatives that may be off-course, and allows senior leaders to determine the best mitigation strategies for getting derailed projects back on track. Is this discussion important? You bet it is. If you ask Charlie Baker, he will tell you this is *the* most valuable service the EPMO can offer *any* organization.

The time allotted at each senior leadership meeting is limited, no more than 10 minutes each session. This forces the PMO to be specific in reporting project issues and requires executives to be concise when determining risk mitigation. The public discussion across senior leadership ensures senior executive accountability. The weekly PMO report forces executive sponsors to be aware of their projects, and to be ready to share course adjustment activities.

Successful Reporting

The key to successful status reporting is not the status definitions, but the ability to get all project stakeholders to report and interpret project status in a consistent and repeatable way. It doesn't really matter what system is used, as long as there is a global understanding across the organization and there is consistent application of each status/definition. The PMO is responsible for maintaining consistent standards and for communicating the standards organization-wide, to ensure they are practiced in a universal and constant manner at all times. "Red," regardless of the specific definition, must mean the same for everyone, all the time. Ensuring standard application of project status often requires regular reminders to both project managers and executive sponsors, to reduce variations in project status reporting. If you don't offer "Orange" as a status definition, don't allow it!

When reviewing project status reports, the PMO often needs to look beyond the summary account for information that may represent a warning sign, such as date changes, past due deliverables, or simply descriptions that either don't make sense or contain enough information to fully assess the project's true status. Don't be afraid to ask probing questions for further assessment. While it is important to examine current status and determine if immediate mitigation is required, it is also important to anticipate pending obstacles. Review longer-term milestones to determine if all are "Green."

HPHC's experience suggests that project status changes from Green to Yellow are typically due to resource allocation issues, inaccurate original estimates, scope changes, or external dependency slippage. A Red status always requires executive intervention. Expect executive sponsors to know what the project risks are and what is being done to mitigate the risks. A sponsor should know what is expected of him/her. Are resources needed? Do roadblocks need to be freed? Is a business decision required?

Walk The Tightrope

The PMO plays a crucial role in communicating business plan activities. The PMO is able to leverage its comprehensive business plan understanding with its neutral position in the organization to effectively keep the company adequately informed about business plan activities. The PMO must maintain honest and trustworthy relationships across the organization to be successful in this role. Often walking the tightrope between supporter and monitor, the PMO will not succeed unless there is corporate acceptance and endorsement of this function. The PMO is charged with monitoring and communicating business plan activities—not to judge corporate performance, but to support corporate success through efficient observation and communication of business plan activities.

Effective communication relies upon simple messaging, supplied in a variety of formats and vehicles. The need for effective communication also carries over to those who must advocate for project management, as we'll see in Chapter 4.

CHAPTER 4

ADVOCATE

I would rather try to persuade a man to go along, because once I have persuaded him he will stick. If I scare him, he will stay just as long as he is scared, then he is gone.

Dwight D. Eisenhower

Advocating project management in any organization requires engagement and commitment from the key stakeholders with the most clout and visibility across the company. There are three groups of players who must drive the acceptance and practice of project management techniques and convention if you hope to achieve cultural buy-in. These key players include the Project Management Office (PMO) (the leader and the staff), senior management, and project managers. Each of these has a distinct role in driving project management acceptance and practice. They must also all work synergistically for their efforts to succeed.

The PMO acts as promoter, campaigner, and upholder of project management practice across the enterprise. Senior executives must be proponents, backers, and spokespersons, while the project managers are the evangelists—always proselytizing for the success of the project.

Project Management Office Advocacy

The PMO employs individuals who act as enablers and facilitators in supporting project success. Regardless of what model your organization's PMO follows, it must establish a culture of discipline by creating processes and tools that support decision-making, improve organizational accountability, and exhibit efficiencies. At HPHC, EPMO staff

50

believes in the four R's: Responsibility, Responsiveness, and Respect in their Relationships. They are biased towards action and common sense, and push cost-benefit decisions. The PMO's objectives are the company's objectives, and they maintain their role through visible support of the company's goals and objectives. When the organization achieves success through timely delivery of projects that come in under budget and produce expected business outcomes, the EPMO has achieved its goals as well. Everything the PMO does every day is in support of this mission.

The PMO has the ongoing challenge of institutionalizing project management practices across an organization. This is achieved through ongoing endorsement of the corporate project management methodology, tool use, and reporting systems. It requires public promotion of project management successes, which is the best way to achieve organizational buy-in. Once these practices are accepted, the PMO has a greater challenge in exhibiting *ongoing* value to the organization. To do this, the PMO must constantly look outside the project management paradigm.

PMOs can experience long-tenured success in any organization by prescribing discipline and process to support evolving business needs. A PMO leader can offer business management recommendations by being diligent in anticipating new business needs, having the ability to modify project management processes to meet other business requirements, and knowing when a process is needed—or more importantly, when it is not—to solve a business problem.

PMO leaders need to establish positive, trusting relationships with executives, project managers and other staff to take the pulse of the organization and to recognize what business problems need to be solved. Sometimes, the PMO may find themselves outside the comfort zone of project management, and in other instances may be thrown together with unlikely associates to meet a business need. This requires flexibility, business understanding, and the ability to partner with others.

At HPHC, the PMO and Human Resources Department are currently working together to address resource management issues. The issues at hand go beyond finding staff to fill vacant project positions; the two departments are establishing a model to effectively find the "right" resources for the "right" projects and to place accountability within business units to develop junior-level staff so they, too, can be placed on project teams. This solves the recurrent problem of always asking for the same people all the time—a model that is unsustainable over long periods. The collaboration between the two departments represents a blending of strengths to produce a more productive outcome. The Human Resources staff applies their knowledge of workforce management, understands staff core competencies, and holds a general expertise in workforce development. The PMO instills process and structure to reach joint goals according to established deliverables and in accordance with deadlines. Their union produces a valuable outcome for the organization as a whole: introducing a corporate model of efficient and effective resource management in support of business imperative activities. This is a perfect example of where the PMO has partnered with an unlikely collaborator to meet a business need.

According to Deb Hicks, VP, Human Resources at HPHC, there are two critical components of success when it comes to PMO promotion. The necessary elements include "access" and "people." "Senior leadership shows value to the PMO and thus gives 'voice' to the PMO by allowing critical access and accountability around the business. This includes access to top leadership meetings, and assignments of roles and responsibility to the PMO." Hicks believes this model works only when people in the PMO exhibit the ability to listen, adapt, and roll up their sleeves as necessary to support business needs.

Hicks also knows a successful PMO requires a certain group of individuals—people who are not in it for themselves, but for the overarching success of the organization. "People who are driven by power and hierarchy are not likely candidates for PMO success, unless that is the dominant culture of the organization. At HPHC, the culture is one of collaboration and thus, the PMO must be able to work and behave in that manner."

A triumphant PMO leader is one who continually seeks opportunities for overall business plan success. This individual must publicly support the cause of the PMO and make it apparent to the organization as a whole how and why the PMO lends value. She must be dedicated to project management discipline, intuitive about organizational need, and tireless in finding creative solutions. Regardless of how long a PMO has been in place at any organization, its future depends upon its ability to constantly deliver value-added opportunities for ongoing business accomplishment.

PMO Support Staff

Ongoing support of project management mastery is critical to the viability of project management at any organization. Continuous growth of project management as a core competency is achieved through ongoing endorsement of an organization's project management methodology through PMO staff.

When establishing a PMO, PMO staff must advocate for the value and benefit of project management practice. A company does not need to be in crisis for PMO staff to successfully advocate the value; in fact, any organization that perceives project management as extra work is missing real opportunities. PMO staff must convince others that project management is a means of getting the work done efficiently rather than an administrative burden.

Bob Sullivan (previously introduced in Chapter 1) has spent an inordinate amount of time advocating project management at HPHC. Sullivan recalls that when HPHC's PMO initially introduced project management requirements, "the immediate challenge of introducing a project 'charter' and status reports to the organization was incredibly difficult. The objective was to bust the perception of the project teams and sponsors that it was 'extra work.'"

Sullivan believes the trick for getting early buy-in is the PMO's ability to demonstrate—in a way staff can see, touch, and feel—that the new requirements are necessary. "The focus must be on the value of the practice and on proving that what is being asked of them does not actually represent additional effort. It must be presented so people understand the project management discipline will not keep them from actually doing the project, but will make the work easier and produce better results." Once staff understands the direct correlation between project management practice and successful results, they will quickly adopt the practice on their own. This is true regardless of organizational state—everyone seeks new opportunities to get the job done faster and better, in a predictable way. The last thing staff want is new administrative burden dumped on them. Sullivan believes that by establishing the project management methodology slowly, with the insertion of only a couple of forms and processes, and active campaigning throughout, a PMO is able to show the project teams the value of these efforts. "We used wins to establish the maxim that 'project management isn't *extra* work; for project teams—it *is* the work.'"

Acting as project management ambassadors, HPHC's EPMO staff offers ongoing support, guidance, and counsel to the business as a whole. No longer limited to pure project management activities, EPMO personnel offer business meeting facilitation, problem solving, training, and processes redesign support.

Careful selection of PMO staff is critical. Successful advocates must have a strong technical understanding of project management practice and also be exuberant about what they do. Members of the PMO must fully commit to the practice of project management, in every way.

Ron Parello, PMP, is a member of HPHC's EPMO. Parello has many years of experience managing large, complex projects, but was looking for a change when he joined HPHC. He did not consider himself a "teacher," but was intrigued by the notion of sharing his project management expertise with others, and quickly found he had a lot to offer. In fact, Parello now realizes his calling is not managing projects, but guiding and supporting others through successful project management activities. He is dedicated to delivering topnotch support for all project stakeholders who seek his support.

"It's very rewarding to teach project management fundamentals to people who are new to the discipline," Parello notes. "Most people use project management techniques in their daily lives without having the vocabulary and structure that a formal project management methodology provides. It's great to see the lights go on in people's heads as they come to understand that the HPHC Project Management Approach simply puts language, structure, and discipline to fairly intuitive and very logical concepts."

Case Study

Parello provided ongoing support to Jim Thrasivoulos, PMP, the project manager assigned to the Vendor Fulfillment initiative. Jim was new to HPHC; he joined the organization only two months before being assigned to manage the priority project. Jim's background was management consulting, business process engineering and project management in high tech companies. Unlike previous workplaces, Jim found the culture at HPHC to be different—primarily due to the positive support offered through HPHC's EPMO. "I was informed about HPHC's PMO office and went to meet them to hear about the approach, support systems and resources including methodology training and organizational process assets, such as project databases, project templates, guidelines and historical project information. I found the PMO very helpful and quite eager to support project managers."

Thrasivoulos describes his first encounter with HPHC's PMO as a welcomed opportunity, "After I met with the project sponsors and learned about the scope of the Vendor Fulfillment project, I was told that a PMO representative would be available to consult with me through the project phases. Being new to the job, this was a great way to get the project off to the right start. Ron's project management knowledge, combined with his enthusiasm for the profession, enhanced my success while managing such an important project."

HPHC's EPMO staff support the organization through an integrated offering that includes both the science and the art of project management. They maintain this tightrope balance by focusing all their efforts toward the overarching goal of supporting project success. They act as PMO liaisons, partnering with project managers assigned to corporate priority initiatives. The liaison follows the project from inception to close, maintaining a delicate balance between project support and project monitoring. This unique role requires project management office staff to be as proficient in the technical aspect of project management as they are in relationship management—often a difficult balance to maintain. Because HPHC's PMO acts as a support function to the organization, it seeks individuals who are seasoned project managers and who enjoy helping others in the profession.

Beginning with the 1999 turnaround, continuing through HPHC's re-emergence as a strong health plan, and now in their current challenge of managing multiple lines of business and re-branding themselves, project management has been a constant in Harvard Pilgrim's culture. It is something HPHC is very proud to have refined to an art. The results of project management at HPHC are clear; PMO staff are delighted with what project management has done for HPHC to date and believe the possibilities are endless through continued project management advancement. PMO staff must be fully dedicated to the ongoing evolution of project management and must be willing to promote their project management beliefs to others in a supportive and facilitative manner. PMO support staff must be hand-selected; it is critical to choose individuals who hold both technical project management expertise as well as the strong character traits needed to support organizational demands.

HPHC's PMO staff speaks internationally and nationally to share best practices with others. They even consult from time to time with other organizations and local governments. They have found it is equally important to advocate the practice of project management outside the organization, as external networking allows HPHC to trade best practices. They have found it does not matter where you discuss project management—everyone struggles with similar challenges, is hungry for answers, and seeks success. Members of HPHC's PMO take great pride in sharing the company's story, lending advice to others, and providing solutions to organizational challenges. HPHC's PMO has, over time, proven the power of project management with real results.

Senior Executives and Organizational Commitment

Executive sponsorship has been identified as one of the greatest contributors to success when managing change, while the lack of that sponsorship is probably one of the greatest reasons for failure. Sponsors must be visible and active, both in their ongoing actions in support of project management as an organizational practice and in their role supporting specific projects. Both roles require commitment and engagement; senior sponsors will not succeed as advocates if they do not maintain both.

Senior leaders play a critical role in the introduction and acceptance of project management in any organization. In fact, their endorsement, or lack thereof, will direct project management to succeed or fail. Senior executives are always under the spotlight. They must practice what they preach to gain staff acceptance. Senior managers who preach project management but do not practice it will lose credibility; they must lead by example. To achieve corporate buy-in on project management practices, senior executives must exhibit project management knowledge, display acceptance, and be enthusiastic.

Dave Segal (previously introduced in Chapter 1) has sponsored a number of priority initiatives for HPHC over the past five years. During this time, he has mastered the role of executive sponsor by maintaining a consistent level of involvement and knowledge of his projects without getting bogged down with details. He allows his project managers to freely manage projects to success and is able to maintain the balance of knowing when to step in—or not—when the project is in trouble. Segal believes his endorsement of project management is necessary for his division to succeed. "It is not just an approach to work, it must be a corporate way of life and it must be engrained in the culture of the organization." Segal believes "it is the obligation of every senior leader to become a project management zealot."

The easiest way for upper management to display this behavior is by showing an interest in projects, participating in project team meetings, extending support to projects in need, and acknowledging project successes. When a business leader encounters a project manager in the elevator, he or she should ask how the project is going; lend a hand if the project is in trouble; or reveal enthusiasm if the project recently hit a key milestone. It does not take a lot of effort or time to show interest and to promote enthusiasm. It is amazing how a senior executive's well-chosen comment can bolster a project manager's confidence and spirit during a quick elevator ride.

Equally important to the success of project management at any organization is senior executives' willingness to exhibit public displays of endorsement. One example of how executives support project management at HPHC is through their regular appearance at the annual project management awards ceremony. This event is a way to publicly acknowledge the importance of project management at HPHC; celebrate the role of project managers, project teams, and project support roles and reward them for their efforts. Their track record of project management accomplishment and HPHC's future anticipated accomplishments are the sources of inspiration for these awards.

This awards program is important because the project managers, the teams, and the support people too often go unnoticed—probably because they have their heads down, working to make HPHC the great health plan that it is. HPHC is in its sixth year celebrating past and future project management successes, and it has become an event of stature and respect. The winners of the "Excellence in Project Management Award" are members of an elite group, so it is imperative that senior managers are involved in presenting project management awards and visibly support project management.

Project Nourishment

Executive sponsors responsible for a specific project must engage early and often to successfully nourish project success. They must be familiar with project management disciplines, know the organization's project management methodology, and be aware of key project management tools. Most importantly, they must understand and accept their role as executive sponsor and be held accountable in a real, measurable way for the success of project and business outcomes.

Most executives are not fully aware of their role as project sponsors, and as a result, look to the project team to implement without them. This creates an interesting and awkward chemistry, as most project teams assume sponsors know what to do and know when to insert themselves. Ironically, many sponsors assume they will be called upon if needed, thus setting up a vicious cycle of unmet needs on both sides.

At HPHC, executive sponsors approve projects—from the project goals through the project closing. They are the high-level business leaders who publicly support the project's efforts and, in this role, provide leadership and vision for the project team. The executive sponsor is responsible for approving and signing the project scope statement. She removes corporate barriers to project success, makes strategy decisions, and communicates, communicates, communicates.

Responsible for successful project completion, the sponsor must fully understand the project's goals, the targeted business outcomes, the major deliverables, and the associated deadlines. She supports project-funding processes. She monitors project activities and manages the expectations of who will do what, based upon the project's unique needs.

Establishing clear roles and responsibilities among the project's key stakeholders and team members is one important role of an executive sponsor. If you are an executive sponsor, be specific and direct with your project manager. Do not assume your project manager knows how you operate or will be able to anticipate your expectations. Even if you have worked with the project manager in the past, the character of each project is unique, oftentimes requiring new roles and responsibilities. Remember, there are no hard and fast rules; simply sit down and figure it out. Roles should be defined based upon the unique needs of each project.

Here are a few key questions to consider when defining roles and responsibilities:

- Before you signed off on the scope document, have you questioned the "documented" why, how, what, and who?
- Do you have a process in place where you access/read the project status reports?
- Do you have a standing meeting scheduled with your project's management teams?
- Have you and your project's management team sat down to discuss roles? Who "owns" the project's major decisions?
- Have you established mechanisms for reporting project progress?

- How (and when) are you made aware of schedule slippage or new risks to the projects you sponsor?
- Have you established ground rules regarding changes to scope, schedule, or resources?
- How do you get involved in "change management" for your projects?

Your project manager and project team will be under great duress to complete significant work under tight deadlines. It is your responsibility to be in touch with your project team on a regular basis. Ongoing support and promotion of the team's work will generate much-needed enthusiasm. This is particularly important for project teams responsible for generating significant change or thrown together for an extended period of time. The executive sponsor must show ongoing endorsement of the team's efforts and accomplishments. This can be easily accomplished through spontaneous visits to the project team, writing brief messages of support and encouragement, and participating when the project team schedules mini-celebrations for meeting major milestones. Show regular support throughout the project lifecycle—do not be visible only at the start and the end of the project, as this will not inspire project team members.

One essential role in supporting project success is ensuring project staffing is in place early on. With most organizations being resource-constrained, executive sponsors can best support the project by actively championing the "right" resources. This requires knowledge of project needs, recognizing the essential competencies needed to support the project, and awareness of the critical due dates. Building a coalition of sponsorship with senior executive peers will also help find the best staff to support the project's requirements.

Project Managers

Project managers are the most valuable assets within a project management-centric organization and they are also the most vulnerable. The majority of project managers live in a matrix environment, which means they are accountable for getting people to deliver for them, even though those people do not directly report to them. They are on the hook for successful project delivery. They are "it" for managing all aspects of the project, from technical planning to team management. Is it quite an unenviable position to be in. Organizations often misunderstand how much is required of project managers to get the project delivered according to scope, budget, and deadline in such a demanding environment.

Project managers must endlessly advocate for their project. This means identifying the "right" resources for the project, requesting appropriate funding for the project, and raising the flag early for help if the project runs astray. Project managers must be proficient communicators, skilled negotiators, and artful organizers. As HPHC assumed a cultural acceptance of project management, project managers no longer needed project management principles forced on them—they demanded it of themselves. As they delivered their projects with remarkable success, they proved that project management worked. They adopted the practice and techniques as their own, working through their own issues, providing their own rigor and bestowing their own motivation. HPHC project managers espouse advocacy for their projects. They know what their projects need and they are not afraid to seek it. A victorious project manager seeks endless support to achieve project success and knows how to navigate the corporate universe to clinch project closure.

Case Study

Jim Thrasivoulos was relentless in advocating for the Vendor Fulfillment project. Given the aggressive due dates, he had little time to contemplate how to best employ his project team; they simply needed to deliver quickly in order to hit critical deadlines. Thrasivoulos promptly deployed a "just in time" strategy to efficiently leverage needed resources. He carefully managed team and vendor meetings by having appropriate stakeholders, subject matter experts, and vendors participate in meetings only for their portion of the meeting agenda. While this may not be the optimum way to manage a project team, it was the best solution for Thrasivoulos at the time—he was able to get the "right" folks in the meetings at the "right" time, enabling him and his project team to maintain momentum while racing to the implementation finish line.

Reaching this level of success is not easy. Project managers must feel empowered to manage their project, be permitted to make decisions, and have authority to delegate to others. Not only do project managers need to be proficient in the technical practice of project management, apply standard tools according to methodology requirements, and report project status in an honest and proactive fashion, they *also* need to know how to navigate their organization, manage relationships within their project team, and establish alliances outside the organization, often reaching out to external clients and vendors. From the moment a project manager is assigned to a project, she must advocate for its successful completion. This requires full knowledge of the project's goal, how it aligns with the strategic vision, and the organizational impact if the project succeeds or fails. Her knowledge of this must be conveyed in everything she does while managing the project.

May Joyce (previously introduced in Chapter 3) has filled a number of roles at HPHC, all in support of project management in one form or another. She has held positions in the EPMO as well as within the business; her current position is in Finance Operations, where she is responsible for managing a number of projects and process redesign efforts. Joyce believes the greatest challenge for project managers is managing expectations. "One of the biggest responsibilities of a project manager is to manage expectations. You are managing the expectations of the executive sponsor, the project team members, the project team members' supervisors, senior leadership of the organization, and the PMO."

Joyce has been on both sides of the fence at HPHC, originally as an EPMO consultant responsible for supporting and monitoring other project managers, and now, as a project manager responsible for successful project delivery. She believes the best way to manage everyone's expectations is through communication. "Communication is an integral part of this. Understanding what tone and communication method works with all of the key stakeholders to advocate for the resources that lead to the project's success is a huge undertaking in any organization." Joyce does not believe this skill is easily learned, as much of it relies upon intuition. However, she is convinced project managers can improve this skill through practice and experience. "Good communication comes with constant application of different communication techniques. It is always better to start out by over-communicating the project needs; a project manager who is not comfortable articulating the project needs will never fill the project requirements."

Endless Advocacy

It is naive to believe advocacy is a temporary, short-term activity. Even in organizations where project management is mature and accepted, it requires ongoing promotion to retain value. The PMO must drive the championing of project management, and support ongoing behavior as part of its daily activities. PMO staff must always seek new ways to promote the inherent value of project management in support of organizational success. Senior executives must stimulate individual and corporate project successes through public endorsement of both the cultural acceptance of project management as well as the individual project successes. Project managers must never cease to find ways to deliver successful project results, both by timely completion of project deliverables and ensuring the project delivers what it set out to accomplish.

Stakeholders can maintain their advocacy positions by combining their knowledge of project management with their continuous pursuit of results. In Chapter 5, we'll explore what type of project management understanding is needed.

CHAPTER 5

UNDERSTAND

An investment in knowledge pays the best interest.

Benjamin Franklin

The simplest way to gain cultural acceptance of project management in any organization is by promoting thorough understanding. Business leaders and staff alike must all understand the value associated with implementing project management practices. More importantly, they must comprehend the relationship of project management activities to realizing business achievement. Creating a leveled understanding across any organization requires thoughtful consideration of key stakeholder needs and recognition of their roles within a project-centric environment. A thoughtful plan is required to educate each constituency accordingly. Each stakeholder has a unique role in defining project success, whether it is the project management organization (PMO), executive sponsors, project managers, or project team members. Each player must hold an understanding of project management methodology, knowledge of organizational requirements, and an appreciation of how each project management activity contributes to the choreography of project success.

It's possible to establish project management understanding through a simple plan. Such a plan involves isolating each constituency, assessing what each group needs to know to support project management, and most importantly, recognizing how the level of their understanding will effect project success. Establish and maintain an educational plan by recognizing the points of pain for each player and creating a program that sets out to address each pain or need. This requires a delicate balance so you do not overload players, yet you provide a level of understanding for each group so they are successful in fulfilling their roles. Once you define a comprehensive training program, overlay additional developmental programs to further strengthen project success; include developmental support in negotiating skills, organizational and time management practice, and communication techniques (written and verbal).

Project management training was crucial to the start-up success of HPHC's PMO in 1999. As the portfolio of projects has evolved to become more complex, longer in duration, and more cross-functional, project management understanding has become more important to HPHC. Project management training programs must be designed with the flexibility to meet such changing needs. This means you must construct adaptable training programs that gradually expose staff to more in-depth levels of project management knowledge, as required. Offer versatile training that enables project stakeholders to apply their knowledge in a more comprehensive, results-producing fashion; help them leverage project management tools better and create new processes and techniques to manage projects differently.

The challenge for any PMO is to establish the "right" selection of training programs to initially develop project management competency and also have the ability to evolve the training plan to meet changing needs. Having a training plan that is simple yet flexible holds many benefits: improved teamwork, more efficient project planning, better work quality, and gains in productivity. As training programs evolve and advance, recipient project managers and executive sponsors also gain efficiencies, resulting in more projects coming in on time. Completing projects on time offers many benefits. When a project delivers ahead of or on schedule, it is apt to produce a more valuable return on investment, and the project team staff can then be released faster to get back to their regular jobs on the front lines. Faster project manager turnaround also allows the limited number of project managers to be assigned to the next project more quickly. With ongoing, more advanced training, HPHC has seen the number of projects finishing on time increase substantially.

In addition, the training is touching customers. Because many projects are focused on operations and process improvements, they improve the experience of HPHC's customers. The more staff know, the better they perform, enhancing overall outcomes for both the organization and its customers.

HPHC's EPMO offers a number of in-house training programs. These range from basic project management training to more advanced levels of training, and they focus on different audience requirements. Training is offered through different venues, ranging from traditional classrooms to informal brown-bag sessions. They also leverage technology and offer learning opportunities through video web conferencing and e-Learning channels. Offering variety within an educational program acknowledges that people learn best in different environments and in different ways. It also exhibits an appreciation for how busy people are—classes are designed to offer enhanced understanding efficiently, with the objective of increasing knowledge quickly, enabling staff to get back to delivering project success.

Because EPMO staff leads the educational efforts, they must constantly upgrade their own level of understanding and continuously gauge organizational needs to recognize what additional training is required. This requires EPMO staff to constantly challenge their own level of understanding; the staff must be proficient in both the technical application of project management techniques and the "soft" skills required to support project success. Once again, this requires careful scrutiny of EPMO staff—you must seek individuals who hold solid experience in project management and who also have a desire to grow and develop others. This is particularly important for EPMOs that act as a central support arm for their organization. Offering project support services, training, and consultation to project managers who reside within business units across the enterprise requires EPMO staff to be proficient in a wide variety of project management techniques.

HPHC refers to project management as the "accidental profession." Many of HPHC's project managers started as subject matter experts and then, through their developed knowledge of the business and their ability to realize results, they were selected to manage projects. This was especially true in 1999, before project management was recognized as offering business value and before it experienced a career explosion. Initial training programs at HPHC were focused on developing project management competency for a very inexperienced audience—many people found themselves thrown into project management with little or no previous experience in this area. This was true for all stakeholders—executive sponsors, project managers, and project team members alike were unfamiliar with project management practices and tool use. This required a training program that provided a foundational understanding of project management. Over time, however, training programs have evolved dramatically, as new project managers are hired with strong project management knowledge and training, thus raising the bar on training requirements.

Foundational Understanding

Any organization looking to establish project management should focus on foundational training first, to establish project management competency and also to educate staff about your organization's methodology. As soon as HPHC established its own project management methodology, the PMO designed a Project Management Approach course. This course introduces HPHC project management methodology, including its lifecycle, processes, workshops, and templates. It contains helpful tips, techniques and tools, and best practices. Attendees participate in a detailed case study with exercises, giving them immediate, hands-on exposure to HPHC's project methodology and tool set. The course helps students understand the importance of the project management methodology used at HPHC and helps them learn how to apply it to enable project success. The two-day course is offered to all project managers, project coordinators, and anyone else highly involved in project work or interested in entering the project management profession. In spite of the existence of a mature project management model at HPHC, the class never struggles to find participants.

Ron Parello is the lead instructor for HPHC's Project Management Approach Training. As you may recall from Chapter 4, Parello did not believe himself to be a "trainer" when he joined the company. Yet, he quickly exhibited pride in ownership. He promptly identified ways to make the course more invigorating, and created a better learning experience for attendees by inserting new visuals, expanding group exercises, and adding his dynamic personality to the course delivery. Once again, Parello's passion for the profession and his newfound comfort with training helped him make the foundational training popular across the organization. Inexperienced project managers and those who are simply curious about the profession are always eager to enroll.

Heidi Aylward recently participated in Parello's class. She was initially introduced to project management through her contributions on a number of project teams, as a subject matter expert. Over time, she developed a keen interest in advancing her knowledge of project management practice. In September, Aylward accepted an entry-level project manager position within HPHC's Customer Service division. Aylward believes the HPHC Project Management Approach training provided the foundational training she needed to succeed in her new role. "Before accepting my new role, I never really thought of project management as a discipline. I gained a good understanding of HPHC's project management methodology, its tool set and supporting processes." Now leading her own projects, Aylward is able to apply the knowledge she gained from this training. In fact, she is eager to further her advancement by attending additional project management courses.

Parello believes the HPHC Approach course is equally important to expert project managers newly hired into the organization. He is enthusiastic when he describes the experience of teaching those in the know. "Even people at an expert level of project management knowledge benefit from and enjoy the class. Not only is it a great refresher on the basics of sound project management practices, it also provides people with the key survival skills for the culturally specific adaptations of the Project Management Institute's (PMI) standards employed at HPHC. It's exciting to see experts and novices work together effectively (and 'speaking the same language') as their teams complete the case study exercise during the two-day class. The end result is that they all leave the class with the ability to participate in, or lead, project teams." Parello believes the HPHC Approach training has increased HPHC's rate of project success.

Executive Training

Senior executives and upper management also require foundational knowledge of project management methodology, and they must understand their role in supporting project success. At HPHC, Executive Project Management seminars are offered each year to senior leaders who are focusing on their role-based requirements as executive sponsors. Seminar topics vary, depending upon need and the type of projects in the portfolio each year. For example, a portfolio that includes many projects containing business process redesign will warrant executive training to support business change activities. Executive sponsors for projects containing significant technology should have a general sense of what is anticipated for such projects and be able to recognize how to best provide oversight for them. The key to successful executive training involves selective focus on topics that promote executive sponsor roles and responsibilities.

Almost all Executive Project Management seminars contain basic review elements in line with simple foundations of project management, both in general and at HPHC. A review of roles and responsibilities is always included, to ensure new business leaders understand and appreciate their role in supporting project success. Other executives simply need to be reminded from time to time, so as not to lapse in their sponsorship responsibilities. The value of these seminars is priceless. It allows the EPMO to retain a strong presence among senior executives, enables executives to enhance project management practices, and establishes a mutual respect and appreciation for collaboration and the need to change and evolve.

As a member of HPHC's senior executive leadership team and an executive sponsor to many priority initiatives, Dave Segal has participated in a number of the Executive Sessions at HPHC. He believes training for executive sponsors is a critical component of ensuring a robust and effective project management culture. In the end, it is the executive sponsors who own the scope, resource allocations, and the ultimate accountability for the initiative's success. Segal believes the project is more likely to achieve its ultimate objective when the executive sponsors know how to guide the crafting and management of scope, allocation and management of resources, and clear the barriers the project managers and team may encounter. In his view, without training in the project management approach, executive leaders will have difficulty meeting their obligations to ensure that corporate objectives are met. "Executive leaders who are not trained cannot manage the scope of the project, resulting in project failure."

Leveled Training

Training programs for project managers constantly evolve, depending upon the nature of the portfolio, the turnover of project management staff, and the evolution of the organization in regard to pace and change. The EMPO analyzes project success metrics at HPHC and offers leveled training in specific project management activities embedded within HPHC's methodology.

A recent analysis suggested that one of the primary reasons projects fail at Harvard Pilgrim is due to poor project planning. The EPMO now offers a focused training in support of project planning activities, "Conducting the HPHC Project Initiation Workshop and Project Planning Workshop." Students learn how to apply a structured approach to initiating and planning projects, and to recognize why it is essential for project success. The course takes basic project management principles and structures them into "agendas" for application to a project. Some practical application in the use of planning constructs is done in the session, giving participants hands-on exposure. Project managers, project coordinators, and project team leaders who attend this course learn how to prepare for HPHC project initiation and planning workshops, how to conduct successful workshops, and how to document the results of these workshops.

The value of offering this particular course at HPHC is huge. First, it develops project managers to learn a technique for effectively leading project teams through project planning activities. Second, it reduces demand on EPMO staff. The time and commitment to teach project managers "how to fish" frees up EPMO staff so they can provide support in other areas. Once project managers are taught how to facilitate a project planning session on their own, they no longer ask

EPMO staff to provide this service. This supports project manager success through expanded empowerment on their project, and frees up EPMO staff so they can focus on new opportunities.

Software and Tool Training

HPHC has created a number of project management tools specifically designed to support the HPHC project management methodology. Most of these tools are introduced during the Project Management Approach training. However, as new tools are introduced, enhanced, or mandated, project stakeholders must be informed accordingly and be trained in their effective use. Each time a new tool is created or an existing tool is modified, the EPMO must communicate all changes and ensure project managers understand how to use the tools, and how the tools support the project and align to the methodology. HPHC's EPMO offers a number of tools in its project management toolbox; some are required, others are optional. All project managers must know what is in the toolbox and how to use the tools to success-fully support each project. Course offerings can introduce new tools or mandate the use of specific tools.

HPHC requires all project schedules to be maintained using MS-Project software. The EPMO offers a course where students learn basic project scheduling concepts and practical techniques for using MS-Project to manage their projects. The course was designed to pro-vide easy-to-learn techniques, which quickly offer value when using MS-Project as the project scheduler. The course is intended to enable students to use MS-Project successfully and quickly, and to learn such basic project scheduling concepts as how to set up MS-Project, how to get project information into the tool, and how to manage the infor-mation as project requirements change.

Project Manager/Project Leader (PMPL) Sessions

In other instances, minor changes to existing tools can be commu-nicated through brown-bag sessions. Project Manager/Project Leader (PMPL) sessions are offered monthly at HPHC. PMPL sessions were established to create an environment in which project managers can come together and share information relevant to their project, which may also affect another project. This forum promotes the timely sharing of information to better manage interdependent relationships among portfolio projects. It is also a forum for sharing best practices and providing flash updates in support of project success. While these sessions are sponsored by the EPMO, they are not *for* the EPMO. The forum was designed with project managers and project leaders in mind; the EPMO regularly solicits feedback and ideas from PMPLs to make these sessions a valuable use of PMPL time.

HPHC's EPMO does not limit training courses to technical project management practice. Project Management constituencies must develop core competencies in good business practice and develop strong management skills to succeed. HPHC's Meeting Management course is a perfect example of where the EPMO offers training outside the technical confines of project management practice. The objectives of the Meeting Management course allow participants to match the type of meeting to the purpose, learn how to successfully plan and conduct a meeting, and, what to do after holding a meeting. Since much of what project managers do today relies upon rallying team members together and producing updates and results through a meeting format, this is an important skill to have.

Finding Partners

Over the last four years, as the health care industry and HPHC's business became more complex, the company needed more employees who could handle ongoing challenges in this fast-paced industry. However, the limited resources within HPHC's EPMO could not help enough staff move to the next level of project management development. Harvard Pilgrim's EPMO was also concerned that the internal resources were insufficient to support ongoing development of project managers.

It made sense to HPHC's EPMO to partner with others, including outside training resources, for a comprehensive training program. HPHC was and is very focused on growing core competencies in project management and aligning with standard industry project management practices at a higher level than the in-house training could accomplish.

HPHC decided in fall 2004 to partner with Boston University's Corporate Education Center (BUCEC) to offer advanced project management training. Harvard Pilgrim recognized the strong reputation of Boston University's training programs and especially appreciated having a connection with a major Boston-based university. In addition, the Corporate Education Center's project management courses were aligned with HPHC's existing methodology, and offered incredible flexibility in developing the program.

With Boston University as its new training partner, HPHC launched the project management certificate training program. The programs run for 12 weeks, meeting two evenings each week at HPHC offices, and is offered once a year to employees. Through the courses, HPHC staff gains technical knowledge of project management skills that align with industry standards. The program also brings HPHC staff to the next level, which is PMP certification; most project managers today recognize the certification as a valuable addition to their professional development. Some individuals who have participated in the program as project coordinators have since been promoted to project managers. This partnership instills a higher level of self-confidence and gives staff yet another level of credential to support career advancement.

When selecting training partners, identify candidates who can meet your current business needs *and* evolve to meet your ongoing needs. Gina M. Westcott, MBA, Director, Program Operations & Product Development, BUCEC, agrees with this strategy. "The partnership between Boston University Corporate Education Center and Harvard Pilgrim Health Care has developed from a training provider/client relationship to a relationship that enables a sharing of information between both organizations. The partnership has evolved due to a collaborative effort to understand the needs of HPHC and how BUCEC can deliver appropriate training to meet those needs."

When establishing a relationship with an external partner, be sure to articulate short-term and long-term goals, as training must be a joint effort, customized for the client and supported from the top down. BUCEC and HPHC have nurtured their partnership over time into one that enables both organizations to continue to grow and develop their employees. This is a win—win arrangement.

PMP Certification

For those project managers who desire PMP certification, HPHC also offers a PMP Study Workshop. HPHC, in partnership with Perot Systems, organizes and supports a formal class schedule intended to help employees prepare to take the Project Management Institute's *Project Management Professional* (PMP) test and obtain PMP Certification status. The course agenda consists of interactive presentations, forum discussions, test-taking strategies, guest speakers, and sample test-taking. HPHC does not require PMP certification of their project managers; yet many project managers are PMP certified.

According to Mark Jorjorian, PMP, Manager, Project Manager Team at Perot Systems, the volunteer after-work PMP study group is succeeding within HPHC and Perot Systems for three reasons:

- Message of Embracement: As part of a collaborative approach between two organizations, a message is delivered to all project managers within HPHC and Perot Systems announcing upcoming study session. The message is one of compassion and understanding to employees not yet certified: "People currently PMP-certified have walked in your shoes and would like to help those who desire to achieve this professional accomplishment."

- Collective Understanding and Commonality: Informal information sessions are held to introduce perspective participants to the program and to bring individuals together from both organizations to share their respective concerns and questions before starting the program.

- Defining a New Community and Embracing Unity: The program offers a comfortable environment for the project management community. As participants share study strategies, a commonality emerges; the commonality quickly turns into unity, resulting in proactive support of each person's goals and achievements.

The Soft Stuff is the Hard Stuff

Harvard Pilgrim's EPMO also partners with its own Human Resources Department in addressing soft skill development for project managers. The two departments periodically survey project management staff to identify areas for development. Some of the areas evaluated include "How to Influence Without Authority," "Motivating Others When Times Get Tough," "How to Give Constructive Feedback," and "How to Negotiate for Results." The survey results help the two departments design and/or offer courses to meet prioritized development needs.

HPHC's Team Leadership Program is a perfect example of how HPHC addresses soft skill development for project managers. The two-day course is designed to help project managers and team leaders with tools to effectively lead a cross-functional team at Harvard Pilgrim Health Care. Upon successful completion of the program, project managers will be able to implement an effective team launch; align team culture and themselves to achieve business results; and utilize the best tools for decision-making, conflict resolution, communication, and team accountability. The course also guides project managers through a process to develop a team action plan for effectiveness. HPHC offers this learning opportunity to those who have team leadership responsibilities and will utilize the tools to further support team effectiveness in achieving business results. For HPHC project managers, it further supports project success.

Successful PMOs must continuously design new courses or affiliate with external partners to offer project management and leadership training, to further develop project management competency. These ongoing efforts are important, as they further solidify the Project Management career path.

Organizations must recognize the need to develop employees for individual growth; individual growth globally supports organizational success. Vary your training in depth, scope, and delivery according to audience need. Leverage a multi-channel approach, such as eLearning, to recognize project stakeholders' demanding priorities and schedules. Extend tiered offerings that keep audience members engaged and enthusiastic about learning. You can accomplish this through a comprehensive menu of workshops, seminars, forums, and brown-bag sessions. Global understanding of project management is a crucial ingredient for project success. Project stakeholders who understand the fundamentals and elements of project management can also appreciate how systemized practices further support project success. Let's explore the value of systemized project management practices in Chapter 6.

CHAPTER 6

SYSTEMIZE

"If you don't know where you are going, any road will take you there."
Lewis Carroll, *Alice in Wonderland*

The project management profession has experienced dramatic growth over recent years. Yet, formal recognition and practice of project management in organizations has not reached the same levels. Based on conversations with business leaders who attended project management industry conferences over the past two years, it seems virtually every organization today conducts some type of project management activity, whether they recognize it or not. A little more than half of all companies do not have criteria for defining project success, and many do not track the benefits of their projects. Most organizations have chaotic, non-repeatable project management processes—they manage project success more by chance than by directive. And only a small number of all companies actually invest the time and the energy in tracking the accrued benefits of their internal projects over a multi-year period.

When there are disconnects between business strategy, project selection, and project execution, business benefits are primarily driven by functional silos and do not necessarily head in the same direction. When there is limited repeatable capability for selecting and managing projects and reporting project performance, there is no real global understanding of how well an organization is achieving its goals. If there's not enough follow-through with consistent reporting on tangible business benefits, an organization won't be able to assess its return on investments.

HPHC's Dave Segal knows leaders need to realize that if different methodologies are used across the company, there is no way of determining how the entire portfolio is really doing. Different methodologies might lead to different sets of answers around success—even though the terminology may be the same. Segal says with conviction, "A common methodology allows you to optimize resources across your organization by understanding when a project (or set of projects) will finish, thereby making resources available for other projects. This optimization cannot just happen without a corporate methodology."

Harvard Pilgrim knows projects fail when there is poor communication, skills are mismatched, or there are resource shortages. The results of these failures usually represent project costs being higher than expected and projects taking too long to finish. Alternately, HPHC realizes project success when there is a high degree of end-user involvement, when executive management actively supports a project, when realistic expectations are set, and when there is accountability. Project success is further promoted through effective communications, efficient risk management, and through a hard-working, focused project team. Efficient operational handoffs are also a key success element.

Systemizing project management practices, project activities, project reporting and project results is the only way to keep an organization sane through it all. Systemizing offers a method to manage the madness and a sure way to achieve business goals.

Project Management Systemization

Project management has many benefits, but begins with a disciplined approach to the prioritization, selection, and successful delivery of projects that support the organization's mission and strategy. A project portfolio management process aligns and prioritizes projects with business goals; a project management methodology offers repeatable processes to manage the work. It relies on a set of methods and tools to answer such questions as, "Why, What, How, Who, and When?"

Designing a common project management approach ensures alignment with overall business success, prioritizes projects to meet strategic goals, and focuses resources on business priorities. Organizations work more efficiently through repeatable, predictable practices; standardized practices allow you to learn from past experiences in a simple, predictive way. Systemized practices also allow you to recognize and mitigate project risks easily and produce an audit trail for project activities and accomplishments.

Just ask Armando Rodrigues, who has managed some of HPHC's more complex and challenging projects over the past four years. He believes organizations must instill structure and process in order to succeed. "I can't imagine any successful organization not having a formal structure in place for accomplishing project work." He's convinced there must be "common language used to articulate deliverables and desirable outcomes," so everyone is headed toward the same achievement. Rodrigues adds, "Once you fully appreciate the value that the discipline and methodology bring to the table, you never want to relinquish it."

You must take a multi-dimensional approach to designing a common project management method. This includes project management principles, pre-established processes, a common set of tools and techniques, and directionally supportive training. HPHC's EPMO is responsible for establishing, promoting, and monitoring all aspects of the common approach, both to evaluate its success and identify improvement opportunities.

There is no "right" way to establish a project management approach. The approach must be developed based upon individual business needs, cultural climate, and dissatisfaction with the status quo. Assessing these elements will determine the "right" approach for your organization and the best way to implement it.

At HPHC, for example, it was done backwards, exactly the opposite of what you might expect. The approach was built "bottom up," developing specific solutions to identified problems before introducing a common approach. Given the crisis circumstance, HPHC needed to first track activities associated with the 150-day turnaround campaign—that was the work most important to the organization at the time.

As a result, a project management lifecycle was not introduced first—instead it began with a project reporting process, which rolled up to an executive reporting process. This process was established to solve a critical challenge—how to keep new leadership informed about turnaround activities. The status reporting process then launched a process and forum for issues management. The issues management process was also vital, as many decisions and activities needed to occur at warp speed. This was all enabled with just a few forms and tools—and all accomplished without having designed a lifecycle first! This is contrary to how most organizations would proceed, yet it was the best approach to address HPHC's pain at the time.

Obviously, not all organizations are seriously ill when they recognize project management is the right remedy. In fact, most organizations should think of project management as a daily vitamin that prevents them from becoming sick. However, the challenge is to evaluate and diagnose "what, why, and where does it hurt?" and to conduct a thorough examination before prescribing the proper treatment. This is why the institution and evolution of project management methodology should be thoughtful. If a project management methodology is injected too quickly, the organization may receive too large a dose.

Methodical systemization requires a multi-year plan focused on project management discipline in its simplest form, and with methodology enhanced according to a focus on the organizational need—not the facility, the theory, or the grandeur of the solution. The plan should aim at the greatest pain first. Be patient with your plan, as it will take three to five years to fully implement a project management culture.

The exact sequence for establishing a project management model is not important, but establishing the right sequence for *your* organization is. Project management methodology should not be built for its own sake; it should be gradually designed to solve the problems being experienced. Cultural acceptance is equally vital; without it, the PMO, regardless of model, will fail.

Sandy Trantina is the PMO Administrator for the Information Systems Department at the Lee County Clerk's Office, located in Fort Myers, Florida. In 2005, she described her unit as "…at the center of a fast-changing technology environment trying to manage many projects initiated to achieve a variety of business goals with competing IT resources and ever-changing priorities." Trantina knew she needed a simple, methodical way to manage projects. She was intrigued after hearing members of Harvard Pilgrim Health Care's EPMO speak at a project management conference; she liked their "simple" philosophy. HPHC was able to provide limited consulting services to Trantina and her staff. "HPHC provided a two-day workshop for our key project managers, which gave us the tools to start two projects—a project management methodology and a project portfolio management approach. Over the next few months, we developed our own methodology modeled after the one in use at HPHC—we simply tweaked the foundational model to meet our own business needs."

Trantina firmly believes in keeping it simple. "Simplicity allows us to focus on promoting team collaboration, communication essentials, planning for and identifying project risks, improved usage of precious IT resources, and providing the project manager with more authority as well as accountability." Over the past year, Trantina and her staff have started to see real results, "Our organization is starting to benefit from improved communications and better planning, and others are learning the terminology used in project management. We are just over a year into having a project management office and we have made great progress."

Establishing reliable and predictable experiences through systematic project management application will gain corporate buy-in, particularly when it can also be done while correlating real, measurable results. When designing a project management lifecycle, keep the plan simple so you don't get lost in the detail. HPHC now has a lifecycle that consists of five phases. The framework is familiar in the profession. Each of the five phases includes "check gates," so project managers and EPMO staff alike can be certain a project is ready to progress to the next phase successfully. At the 30,000-foot level, HPHC's lifecycle looks like this:

HPHC Project Management Lifecycle
...at the 30,000-foot level

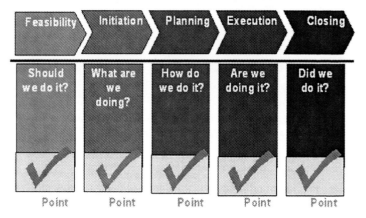

Figure 6-1—HPHC Project Management Lifecycle

Creating a common practice of project management sets universal expectations that can be collectively evaluated for early diagnosis when change is suggested. HPHC's PMO continuously monitors project managers who adhere to HPHC's project methodology, and monitors project success and failures through project management tools and constituency feedback. The PMO is responsible for setting the expectations for project management practice, defining the tools that support the practice, and monitoring the value to the organization through ongoing evaluation of project success.

Introducing new methodology requires uncompromising practice. The PMO is challenged by having to demand methodology adoption without creating corporate alienation. It is important for the PMO to place precise requirements to ensure lifecycle practice. It is more important for the PMO to publicly exhibit the wins associated with the expected standard practice. In other words, everyone who has a role in supporting project management must see visible results from their efforts. Sometimes, simply highlighting the pain is enough to capture attention and obtain buy-in.

HPHC's Days of Disorder

Harvard Pilgrim CEO Charlie Baker describes the disorderly environment evident when he joined the company: "HPHC had a long list of meandering projects that literally had start dates that were years in front of their current status dates. It was amazing. Stuff had been in process forever, even though much of it had 'mission critical' status. This was, of course, bad—for three reasons. First, no one ever expected anything to start and finish on time anymore. Second, no one knew how to count on someone else's work being completed if they needed something for their own work. And three, it totally blew up the ROI and the value of virtually every project that was on the list."

What Baker describes seems to be a common scenario in many organizations today. What is the easiest way to advocate the benefits of project management? Highlight the current environment and note what projects are *not* delivering. As soon as project resuscitation is applied through project management practice and tool use, publicize the results in a big and bold way.

This is a sure way to gain acceptance and change behavior. As soon as project stakeholders see tangible results through improved project delivery, they will readily embrace the practice. As project managers gain proficiency in practice they will adopt the methodology as their own, work their own issues, provide their own rigor and become self-motivated. This will then allow the PMO to back off from the enforcer role and become a service organization.

Build the methodology slowly. It is always easier to add components to the model than it is to subtract them. Methodical construction sets the pace for expectations and allows the PMO to fully evaluate the existing process before making changes or enhancing the current state. This also allows the PMO time to solicit constituency feedback, further strengthening the relationship between the PMO and the business. A PMO that can effectively find ways to identify and gather issues that plague projects will be guaranteed long, successful tenure in any organization. Keeping the plan problem-focused will produce quick wins—another way to acquire and maintain corporate buy-in.

Solutions should be simple and based on project management principles. Concepts such as work breakdown structure, triple constraint, stakeholder management, and best practices manifest themselves in the reality of real-time project concerns. What is the formula for success?

Solution in Response to Problem = Success

And here's the formula for the opposite of success, just as a cautionary note:

Solution to No Identifiable Problem = Administrative Burden and Overhead

Successful systemization requires global commitment. One of the hallmarks of truly successful organizations—those that continually change and improve how they operate to remain competitive—is the ability to quickly and effectively accomplish priority initiatives that cut across traditional organizational silos. Harvard Pilgrim developed an approach to cross-functional project management that, over time, has resulted in a track record of accomplishment that exceeded expectations.

According to Bruce Bullen (previously introduced in Chapter 1), there are two essential ingredients behind HPHC's successful approach to cross-functional project management. "The first is the effective collaboration and work of the project sponsors and project managers running the projects. The second is the infrastructure HPHC has put in place to support and track their efforts." This includes everything HPHC has installed over the past seven years, from a "hub and spoke" support model to project coordination and status review meetings. It also includes numerous tools and communication vehicles and an overall approach to project management based on clear planning, identification of dependencies, swift decision-making, and an imperative for rapid implementation.

Bullen believes that, as the organization continues to change and improve on how it operates, so too will its project management infrastructure and approach. "This approach has served Harvard Pilgrim well and will continue to be the basic process by which HPHC will manage cross-functional work."

The roll-out of a project management office and project management methodology should be built using one process for needs assessment and a separate process for practical application. Balance the needs with solutions for success. Concentrate on what matters (the organizational need) in developing the project management discipline as a methodology.

The Use of Tools

Do not confuse the use of project management tools with project management methodology. Successful project management is not about the tools. It is not even about the content of the tools. It is about thinking, acting, and managing the factors that will determine the project's success. Project management and the discipline of good project management practice have brought significant benefits to many organizations.

Over the past few years, many organizations have turned to enterprise project management software to solve their inability to deliver successful projects. On the surface, this may appear to be a viable solution. The enterprise systems have the ability to produce extensive data regarding project status, risk, and activity. However, in the absence of a solid, dependable project management methodology, the software's bells and whistles cannot produce project success. Unless an organization has become proficient in such activities as project planning, resource estimation, risk management, and change scope management, the data entered into the enterprise system is flawed. Bad data in means bad data out, regardless of how fancy the tool may be. The key to success is using this simple equation:

Solid Processes + Appropriate Level of Software Functionality = Success

HPHC continues to rely upon simple, homegrown tools to support project management activities. The reason for this is, despite well-accepted, widespread project management practice, HPHC can still improve at some of these activities. Additionally, HPHC will never need to reach the level of proficiency required to use certain software. HPHC is not NASA and never will be, so it does not make sense for HPHC to over-invest in project management systems. Always evaluate your options against your needs before making a decision. And remember, investing a lot of money in a new enterprise system before mastering some fundamental project management practices will not provide favorable results.

Today, HPHC has over a dozen tools to support project management activity. Each tool supports a key phase in the project management lifecycle. Some of the tools found in HPHC's tool kit are required for priority projects, while others are available on an optional basis to further support successful project delivery. The tool kit has grown over time, and many tools initially placed in the early tool kit have evolved, based upon project transformation and project team feedback. The idea is to build the tool kit slowly, as too many tools too soon will overwhelm even the most proficient project manager. Limit the number of mandated tools, and require them only when they exhibit verifiable value to the project and the organization—either in project delivery or in project reporting. Too many complicated tools will distract the project manager from what she should be doing. Significant time spent on project administration will cause project manager burnout or lead to missing critical project items.

The most successful tools are those created to address a specific need and likely to last, regardless of project transformation. Tools designed to prevail in spite of project complexity will hold the most value. Develop the tool to eliminate a problem, not to simply support a process. Harvard Pilgrim has a number of tools in its toolbox, all of which were originally designed to solve a particular problem. These tools have also demonstrated long-term value, as they still apply today, in spite of project portfolio evolution. In other words, the simple tools met the needs when the projects were "simple," and many of the same tools meet the needs of "complex" projects today. Here is a quick overview of HPHC's most-utilized tools.

Project Opportunity Statement (POS) Template

The POS is the foundational scope document used by HPHC. This document specifies the business opportunity, the project goals and deliverables, and the expected business outcomes the project will deliver to Harvard Pilgrim Health Care. The executive sponsor reviews and approves the project scope once it is drafted. (Her signature represents the initiation of executive sponsorship accountability.) Once approved, it becomes the foundation for future planning and execution of the project. It also becomes the reference document for questions or resolving conflicts over the project's purpose and scope. As one of the early tools created for the HPHC Project Management Tool Box, it has retained much of its original format and can sustain constant use, regardless of project size, type, or scope. This tool has been so effective that many business units use it for all projects, whether the project is a priority initiative or not.

HPHC's POS consists of seventeen components, all critically important to defining project scope (what's in the box).

1. **Business Opportunity**: The opportunity defines the particular business opportunity or problem being addressed by the project. It contains statements of well-known fact, that everyone in the organization will accept as true.

2. **Project Goal**: A project has one overall goal that concisely summarizes what will be delivered by the project that addresses the business opportunity above. The goal provides a continual reference point for any questions regarding the purpose of the project's direction. For example, "Design and implement XXX system."

3. **Constituents**: This allows you to identify all constituents who are impacted by the project.

4. **Line of Business**: This allows you to designate the line(s) of business impacted by the project.

5. **Scope**: The scope identifies which aspects of the business are to be included in the project and which are to be excluded. It determines what other external influences and impacts (such

as interfaces, customer needs, and regulatory requirements) are to be addressed. This can range from business process scope and business product scope to organization scope, application scope, or "other."

6. **Expected Business Outcomes**: These are the criteria by which the business success of the initiative will be determined.

7. **Major Project Deliverables/Measuring Project Completion**: The deliverable statements define what constitutes project completion. The major project deliverables describe what must be accomplished in order to achieve the business outcomes and reach the project goal. Deliverables should describe what is to be accomplished (i.e., a future state; typically a noun) and an action (i.e., how the deliverable will be delivered; typically an action verb). A planned date and measures of completion help to clarify deliverables.

8. **Major Milestones**: Use this section to document the milestones (events) that must occur in order to reach the deliverables noted in the section above.

9. **Applicable Lifecycle/Methodology**: This allows identification of any other lifecycle/methodology that is required to support project requirements, i.e., product development lifecycle.

10. **Committee Approvals**: Project teams often need to obtain approvals from executive sponsors or steering committees. Such parties are identified here.

11. **Assumptions**: Factors that, for planning purposes, will be considered to be true, real, or certain. This is important, as many noted assumptions represent a risk.

12. **Risks to Project and Contingency Plans**: Risks are factors that may interfere with the project work. For example, internal risks are factors that the project team can control or influence, such as staff assignments and cost estimates. External risks are factors beyond the project team's control or influence, such as market shifts and government action. This

section should include contingency plans (if any risks may be assumed) for addressing those risks.

13. **Dependent Initiatives**: It is important that the project stakeholder understand how this project is linked to other work in the organization.

14. **Core Team Personnel Resources**: Document the skill sets and/or specific people this project will need for its core team. It is important to estimate the extent of commitment necessary for each personnel resource. (Detailed resource requirements for the entire project will be determined after the planning phase of the project is complete.)

15. **Alternates Considered**: Note any other approaches that the team considered when preparing this project. Explain why these alternatives were rejected.

16. **Financial Analysis—Quantitative**: Define the financial impact of the project. If the project is being justified on the basis of financial return, a detailed cost/benefit analysis should be provided.

17. **Authorized to Proceed**: This is where the executive sponsor signs this document, to approve the start of project activities.

RAID Tool Template

The RAID (Risks, Assumptions, Issues, and Decisions) tool was originally developed during HPHC's turnaround to ensure quick action. Originally using just easel sheets and markers, the PMO would force action by documenting action items, owners, and due dates during business imperative meetings. Recognizing this discipline was also needed on project teams, the PMO created the RAID template. It was evolved into a process and tool in response to project teams' lack of discipline and inconsistency in their approach to action orientation.

The RAID tool captures all risks to be mitigated, assumptions to be validated, issues to be resolved, and decisions to be documented. It tracks what action is needed, who is doing it, when it is being done, and the status. The document is housed on a simple Excel spreadsheet and can be used throughout the project lifecycle. Not only does it impose prompt action, it also catalogues all issues identified throughout the life of the project. It can be easily sorted by "open/closed" items and "due dates," supporting action orientation and endorsing results.

RAID (Risks, Assumptions, Issues, Decisions)

Seq #	UID	RAID Code	DESCRIPTION and IMPACT	DATE OPENED	OWNER	ACTION TO BE TAKEN / STATUS / RESOLUTION	DATE DUE	DATE CLOSED
1	1							
2	2							
3	3							
4	4							
5	5							
6	6							
7	7							
8	8							
9	9							
10	10							
11	11							
12	12							
13	13							
14	14							
15	15							
16	16							
17	17							
18	18							
19	19							
20	20							
21	21							
22	22							

Figure 6-2—RAID Tool Template

Project Status Report (PSR) Process and Template

This was the very first tool created at HPHC, and is probably the most valuable and most utilized. The Project Status Report, as previously described, tracks weekly progress on deliverables by project; it identifies risks and mitigation plans, critical for weekly status reporting to the Executive Leadership Team. This is the vehicle employed to indicate the status of overall project health. Weekly project status is shown by a Green, Yellow, or Red indicator to reveal healthy or ailing projects. It is the quickest way to gauge the temperature of a project, and allows project managers to easily summarize project activity and highlight risks or issues.

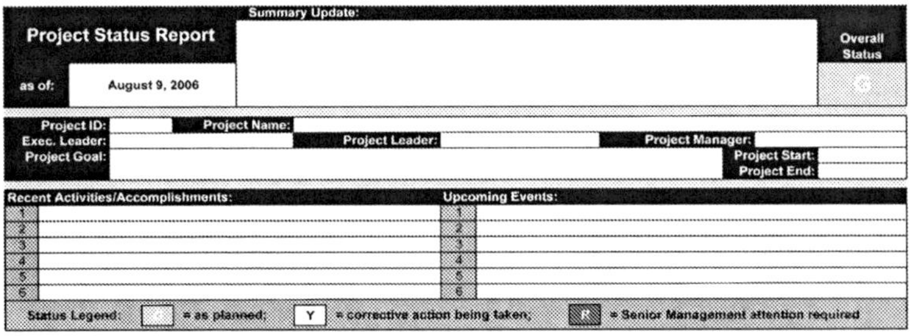

Figure 6-3—Project Status Report excerpt (top)

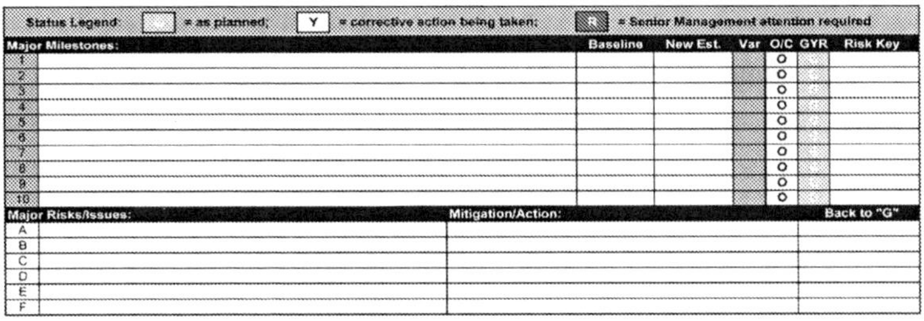

Figure 6-4—Project Status Report excerpt (bottom)

Project Resource Plan (PRP) Process and Template

The PRP tool addresses the pain most familiar to people managing projects—too many projects, too few resources. The PRP identifies resources required for the project, the necessary skill set, and time required by month for the duration of the project. Using the project schedule as a guide, project managers complete the Resource Plan to help them anticipate personnel resources. Each resource requirement will have a specific task or set of tasks to perform, a timeframe in which this must happen, and a level of effort for each requirement. When completing the PRP, project managers indicate which resources have been secured (i.e., have received commitment from line managers) and which skills are still being recruited.

During a quarterly consolidation of individual Project Resource Plans; project managers are asked to submit a "fresh" view of their resource requirements. The EPMO consolidates the information and publishes it back to the organization. This quarterly reassessment allows the organization to anticipate pending collisions, where the same individuals are needed on multiple projects at the same time. This continual refreshing of information allows senior leaders to mitigate resource contention issues before they create serious consequences for the project.

The Quarterly Summary Resource Report contains multiple workbooks, allowing business leaders to sort the data according to their individual business need. The "Name Subtotal" sort seems to be the most popular—it is a quick and easy way for business units to identify when specific employees are over-consumed by project work. Using conditional formatting with Excel also allows the EPMO to point out "over-allocated" staff to business leaders in a position to reallocate staff across projects or identify new resources to meet project requirements. Since the PRP only collects resource requirements associated with project work, functional managers must determine what the data really means, as operational commitments are not calculated.

Project Closing Statement (PCS) Process (also known as Project Closing Workshop-PCW)

The Project Closing Statement helps bring the project to an end. The information from this template is used to help improve the overall environment for project management in the organization. The EPMO updates other project management tools based on the information submitted, and will also provide a central access point for the lessons learned across all projects.

When conducting a Project Closing Workshop (PCW), the facilitator guides the project team members and other stakeholders through a standard project closing process so that all projects are completed in an organized and successful manner. Project closing ensures that the loose ends are addressed and provides a mechanism for documenting and sharing lessons learned. The template includes the following sections:

- Project Closing Checklist—a reminder of the steps needed to close a project
- Project Completion—documents the project completion relative to the expected deliverables
- Business Success—documents the business success of the project relative to the business outcomes
- Lessons Learned—documents lessons learned, what worked and what did not, for use by other projects at HPHC

We will explore the project closing process in more detail in Chapter 10.

Case Study
The Vendor Fulfillment project utilized each of the tools noted above. You will find completed samples and comprehensive details in the Appendix: *A Case Study*.

Project Documentation

Be sure all project documentation is systemized, so both project managers and the PMO can easily keep track of important documentation. Document control is necessary so project teams do not make mistakes by following outdated processes or using old tools. Use a central repository to house all project documentation. Using naming conventions and version control is important, especially if it is coupled with established rules regarding editing rights, assigned accountability, and ownership. Keeping an organized library of project documentation will allow project teams and the PMO to easily access key documentation quickly. It also supports the end user's ability to locate "good examples" of template use and supports reuse of archived information.

An effective project manager uses both art and science to achieve successful project results. The art is the creativity and flexibility to balance the requirements of scope, quality, time, and budget. The science is applying proven, repeatable tools, techniques, and processes to a project. Standardized project management practice and tool use create harmony between the science and art of project management. The magic of project success occurs when you overlay these with solid business processes. Chapter 7 explores such practices.

CHAPTER 7

EFFECT

Action to be effective must be directed to clearly conceived ends.

Jawaharlal Nehru

According to the *Britannica Concise Encyclopedia*, "effect" can be used both as a noun and a verb, meaning "a result" or "bring about a result." The best way to assess the effect of project management on your organization is by monitoring key performance metrics, especially those influenced by project activities. For Harvard Pilgrim, it is clear how project management has affected the organization. The company's ability to recover from a state of imminent collapse and become a prominent health plan was not an accident. The PMO has supported the organization's success by creating processes HPHC has effectively used to select the "right" set of projects and efficiently used in successful project delivery. As a result of the progress made during the turnaround, HPHC is a huge believer in the value of project management, as well as the direct correlation between the adoption and practice of project management and the organization's success.

An organization can realize many benefits through project management: improved teamwork, more efficient project planning, better work quality, and gains in productivity. In addition, as project teams gain efficiencies, more projects come in on time, allowing project team members to be returned to their front-line jobs more quickly. Staff who participate on project teams that identify best practices will take those practices with them when they return to their respective business units. As in the process of osmosis, the business gradually assimilates many of the techniques people learned on project teams and applies them in day-to-day operations. It's clear that the benefits associated with these small, yet effective best practices, when repeated in similar situations outside project teams, can influence enterprise success. This is particularly true in organizations that operate in a matrix environment—a setting that adds a level of complexity when the staff is asked to produce business results without functional barriers getting in the way.

Valuable business practices do not need to be complex to be effective. Over the years, Harvard Pilgrim has identified a number of effective practices, many of which originated on project teams or in support of project success. In some instances, these best practices now support overall business success. This chapter shares some best practices identified at Harvard Pilgrim, which you can easily adapt to meet similar business challenges in your organization.

PMO Liaisons

There are many PMO models, all designed with unique infrastructure to support project management activities. In some organizations, all project managers operate from an EPMO, where they are centrally pooled and assigned to projects as needed. Other companies function with project managers spread across the business; project managers are assigned to a project sponsored by their respective business units. There is no right or wrong model; what works is what's right. Regardless of where project managers reside, they all require central support. It is always the EPMO's responsibility to offer central project management support.

In 2004, HPHC's EPMO identified the need to strengthen central project management support through the introduction of a PMO Liaison role. PMO Liaisons are full-time members of the EPMO and support the tactical execution of the business plan by providing one-stop, consistent PMO contact for the project managers responsible for managing priority initiatives. The one-on-one relationship established between the EPMO consultant (the liaison) and the project manager results in individual oversight from project inception through to project closure. The customized support provides responsive service to project manager needs. Through liaison relationships, the EPMO can better support project managers by providing strong consultative services. The one-on-one relationships create a channel of opportunity for both project managers and liaisons. Project managers receive needed guidance; liaisons identify improvement opportunities for corporate project management methodology and/or tools. Portfolio tracking is also enhanced through these relationships.

PMO Liaisons are assigned to priority initiatives. Liaisons establish relationships with project managers and retain the liaison relationship throughout the lifecycle of the project. PMO Liaisons support project manager needs and monitor all project activities, including providing a "check gate" for projects as they travel the HPHC project management lifecycle. The relationship between the PMO Liaison and project manager is a valuable one for both. The PMO offers consultation and support services to project managers, to ensure they are adequately equipped to handle the rigors of each project. The project manager has dedicated support, through one primary EPMO contact, ensuring continuity throughout the project's duration. The EPMO learns a great deal through the relationship established between the liaison and the project manager.

The PMO Liaison relationship works only when there is a continuous feedback loop. Liaisons must routinely share their experiences and observations with their peers in the EPMO. Their feedback must then circle back to project managers and other project stakeholders so lessons learned are shared with others and project management improvements are realized. Likewise, project managers must feel safe when asking for guidance; they must identify the EPMO as a supportive haven, where they can receive the support they need to ensure successful project delivery. The liaison must provide this support without judgment.

Case Study
Ron Parello, PMP, acted as the PMO Liaison for the Vendor Fulfillment project. He believes his role as a successful Liaison requires a delicate balance between two important, yet sometimes opposing roles. The first, and what he sees as his primary function, is to provide any consulting, coaching, or mentoring assistance to the project manager, in support of achieving project completion. Always meeting the project manager's needs, Parello has a favorite adage, "How High," meaning

the PMO will stretch as high as needed to provide supportive services. Ron views his second responsibility as being an overseer—insuring the appropriate project controls are put in place to allow for the best possible chance of project success. "This monitoring role could be reviewed as an auditor function—this is where we need to use a great deal of tact and finesse."

To successfully provide both services, HPHC's EPMO staff must evaluate each project manager's skills and experience to anticipate the proper amount of support (consulting and monitoring) required. In the case of the Vendor Fulfillment project, Jim Thrasivoulos, the project manager assigned to the initiative, was an experienced project manager, but new to HPHC. To be successful in the Liaison role, Parello needed to quickly adjust to Thrasivoulos' level of project management experience as a seasoned project manager, while insuring he adhered to HPHC's "rules of the road" (following their methodology and tool use).

For Thrasivoulos, having an immediate connection to the EPMO was invaluable. Getting the project initiated, getting all the stakeholders on board, and identifying and committing needed resources were the hardest aspects of launching project activities. Thrasivoulos quickly welcomed Parello's support; the two worked together to establish initiation and planning activities and established meeting agendas and tools to get the project off the ground.

In his Liaison role, Parello supported Thrasivoulos through the Initiation Phase of the Vendor Fulfillment project. In this phase, HPHC conducts an exercise to answer the question, "WHAT are we doing?" Parello made sure the necessary controls were put in place to adequately answer this for the project. He guided Thrasivoulos through the Project Opportunity Statement (POS), which is the foundational document that details all aspects of the project. (This was introduced in Chapter 6). Although the POS has 17 sections to help define project scope, this initial exercise focuses on a process that results in the completion of four sections of the POS tool:

- The Business Opportunity (Why are we doing it?)
- The Goal (What are we doing?)
- The Deliverables (What will we create?)

- Expected Business Outcomes (What is the impact on the organization?)

Once these four sections of the POS were completed, the liaison and project manager teamed together again through the set of activities known at HPHC as the Project Initiation Workshop (PIW). First, the two had a PIW pre-meeting, where Parello worked with Thrasivoulos to establish workshop goals and to identify workshop participants necessary for a successful outcome. The liaison also worked with the project manager on PIW preparation, such as issuing meeting notices, preparing workshop handouts, confirming key attendees, and preparing the meeting room with appropriate set-up and visuals.

Parello offered facilitation services to Thrasivoulos and his team. Acting as facilitator, Parello made sure the project foundation was set and understood by key participants; obtained "buy in" from the organization (through business representation), and established next steps to establish project team endorsement and engagement.

The goals of the Project Initiation Workshop were clear to both:

1. Provide background information on the project (Why we are doing this)

2. Determine what we need to do

3. Plan for the next phase in the project lifecycle (Planning—How will we do it)

Parello and Thrasivoulos accomplished the first goal by communicating the rationale and intent of the project by reviewing the Project Opportunity and Project Goal. The second goal was accomplished by:

- Agreeing on the major project Deliverables, what constitutes their completion and timing;

- Determining the project scope—understanding and documenting the boundaries of the project; and

- Agreeing on the Expected Business Outcomes (impact on specific metrics in the operational environment)

The third goal was accomplished by agreeing on who would be required/assigned to plan the project in the next phase. Parello also assisted Thrasivoulos by establishing a baseline schedule, using MSProject. This was a great help to Thrasivoulos, as he had not used that software tool in some time and was a bit rusty with the application. Given the aggressive schedule, Thrasivoulos and Parello worked together to identify how and where they could leverage their combined strengths to gain traction and deliver project results.

Since HPHC introduced the PMO Liaison role, project manager satisfaction with PMO services has increased significantly. As demonstrated by HPHC's EPMO annual customer satisfaction survey, satisfaction is highest for "responsiveness" and "availability and access." Overall project management consultation and support assistance remains highly rated by project managers, suggesting that the PMO Liaison supports project managers in the way it was intended. The EPMO strongly endorses the liaison role because it has identified many methodology improvements since the program's inception.

Project Plan Reviews

Successful PMOs often endure the challenge of walking a fine line between providing project support and monitoring project methodology compliance. This tightrope walk requires delicate balancing. To be effective in fulfilling both requirements, EPMO staff must be accountable for monitoring project management practice and also be aware of their own failures to deliver to project managers who are being monitored. In other words, they must exhibit transparent humility to be effective.

Irrespective of how the PMO behaves, it does have the dual role of supporting and monitoring project success. In 2001, HPHC's EPMO launched a project plan review process to further strengthen the monitoring role. Because HPHC project metrics showed projects failed due to poor project planning, project plan reviews were implemented to insure project planning was comprehensive and complete before a project is allowed to advance to implementation.

The PMO Liaison conducts a project plan review with each project manager, project lead, and executive sponsor responsible for a priority initiative. The project manager responsible for the project takes the lead in walking the review team through the approach and tools for managing the project. Tools usually include the project scope document (at HPHC, this is called a Project Opportunity Statement [POS]), project resource plan, project schedule, communications plan, and project status reports. The outcome of the review produces a project plan evaluation, documented by the PMO Liaison, which answers the following questions:

1. Does everyone understand the project?
2. Is there a solid communications plan in place?
3. Is the project well documented?
4. Is there a risk-issue management process in place?
5. Are resources secured?
6. Will the project require business process redesign (BPR) considerations?
7. How are interdependencies being managed, i.e., other projects and initiatives?

If action items are identified during the review, the PMO Liaison will work directly with the project manager to complete the necessary steps for finalizing project-planning activities. The review process proceeds much more smoothly when the project manager sends project documentation to the review team in advance of the actual review. The PMO Liaison documents all findings and monitors ongoing project activities as the project advances through the project management lifecycle. Complex, lengthy projects often require a mid-project review, so all project stakeholders have the opportunity to formally review project plan components.

PMO Liaisons also conduct a project closing for project teams, by facilitating "Lessons Learned" workshops. This service offers great value to the project manager and the project team. Allowing the PMO Liaison to guide the project team through a Lessons Learned exercise takes the heat off the project managers—particularly effective if the project manager was not proficient in leading the project or the team.

While most project managers are not overly receptive to the EPMO's review, they have accepted it as standard practice and understand it is a corporate requirement for all priority initiatives. Armando Rodrigues (previously introduced in Chapter 6) describes what it is like, as a project manager, to participate in such a review process, "When project plan reviews were initially introduced at HPHC, I was a bit anxious about what it would be like. After all, the project leadership was going to be present, and I was not looking for someone in the EPMO to tell me I was not doing something right. However, once I discovered the collaborative nature of the process and that the goal was to help me be more successful, I felt more at ease. It quickly became apparent to me that the review process was an ideal way to bring project leadership in sync with project activities and to ensure they understood the purpose of the project, along with the challenges of the project."

According to Rodrigues, who has successfully managed many complex projects for HPHC, the primary reason the review process works is participant engagement. He believes the project manager, project lead, and executive sponsor all need to participate together in order for all project stakeholders to share a common understanding of project scope, schedule, and risks. This is particularly important when working in a matrix environment. "When project leadership comes from different areas of the organization, there are sometimes fewer opportunities to bring everyone together at a critical point during project activities, to make sure everyone understands what is being accomplished. This check gate provides an opportunity for discussion and synchronization."

Some see the review as an opportunity to proactively adjust project activities at a crucial time—before actual implementation begins. Rodrigues describes it this way, "If there is a time to correct something, this is the time. It's better to realize you've selected the wrong tires for your car *before* you purchase them, have them mounted, drive on them, damage your car through a 'wrong' purchase, and then find out you have to buy new tires, since you have already driven on the wrong ones and you can't return them."

Making Meetings Work

"If you had to identify, in one word, the reason the human race has not achieved, and never will achieve, its full potential, that word would be meetings."

Dave Barry

Today's competitive environment forces organizations to be nimble and efficient. More often than not, organizations believe they are being productive through over-use of business meetings. According to the National Statistics Council, 37% of employee time is spent in meetings. Over 11 million meetings are held every day; many do not produce efficient business results, representing lost productivity. We call meetings to inform, we mandate meetings to decide, we hold meetings to analyze, and meetings to assess. All in all, most meetings are unproductive, do not produce business results, and are not an effective use of time.

HPHC quickly learned how to hold effective meetings during their time of crisis. They were forced to gather input from key stakeholders and act quickly in order to remain in business. Before their crisis forced efficiency, they were like everyone else—quite inefficient with the largest investment of all—time. In other words, they were not good at meetings. Over time, HPHC has identified some effective practices to improve the likelihood of conducting effective and efficient meetings.

Set a Standard for Meeting Management

Most organizations do not have a standard model for meeting management. As a result, too many organizations spend too much time in meetings that produce too few results. Organizations can improve by applying these simple steps for establishing standards for effective meeting management.

Pre-Meeting Activities

Meeting preparation requires multiple steps. HPHC highly encourages the following steps to ensure a productive use of meeting time:

1. Create a goal statement and distribute the goal with the meeting agenda. This tells participants the purpose of the meeting up front, so they know why they are coming and the intended outcome.

2. Determine who needs to attend the meeting. Clarify who is a "must have" and who should be invited as back-ups or extra reinforcement. Be clear when you invite your meeting participants. For example, if an invitee cannot attend the meeting due to a schedule conflict, can a representative attend in his/her place? Will the back-up attendee be expected to act with the same level of authority as the original invitee? All these expectations should be clearly stated in advance of the meeting. If key stakeholders (or appropriate representatives) cannot attend, postpone the meeting.

3. Send out the meeting notice in advance. For scheduled meetings where advance notice is available, try to provide at least seven days' notice. If pre-work is required, be specific in stating the requirements. In some instances, detailed instructions may be needed; in other instances, the invitees can attend with little to no advance preparation. Be clear about what you want your participants to know beforehand, or what you want them to bring to the meeting.

4. Pick a neutral location; this is especially effective if the meeting is called to resolve conflicts or solve complex problems. Select a location where participants are unlikely to receive interruptions, if possible. Make certain appropriate seating is arranged, and that equipment and services are ready and working properly.

During a Meeting
Run most meetings according to this simple seven-step guideline:
- Start and finish on time
- Post the meeting's goal/objectives so everyone who attends can see them
- Post and follow a prepared agenda, with assigned time frames

- Establish meeting guidelines and roles at the start of each meeting
- Capture and post "action items"
- Present and evaluate information
- Close with "next steps"

Ending a Meeting

This can be accomplished by simply saying, ten minutes before the meeting is over, "Let's wrap it up, we need to be out of here in five minutes." This gives participants time to organize their thoughts, have a last word, and mentally sum up for themselves what the meeting has meant to them. It also begins the transition to next steps—what actions are needed from this point on and how to proceed. Summarize the proceedings for the group, review the meeting's purpose and ask if it has been achieved, summarize the events, accentuate the positive results, and determine next steps. Deliver closing comments with energy and power. Be sure to thank the participants, include a collective thank-you to the group, and also be sure to recognize those who were key contributors to the meeting's success.

Assessing the Meeting

You may think the meeting was a huge success, but others may leave feeling frustrated and less than appreciative about spending their time without reaching a decision affecting them. Without an assessment, there is no way to determine whether the meeting's purpose was achieved. In its simplest terms, the meeting assessment answers three questions:

- What happened?
- What was accomplished?
- What was not accomplished?

Asking your participants to evaluate the meeting can be done quickly; you do not need to ask each participant to spend lots of time filling out a comprehensive report card when the meeting ends. In fact, the shorter the assessment, the better.

Post-Meeting Activities

Be sure to document and distribute meeting minutes, including action items. This should be done within 24 hours of the meeting, if possible, as prompt meeting follow-up establishes momentum for getting the work done.

"Alpha Meetings"

Getting key participants to convene quickly is a huge challenge for most organizations. Many of the "must have" contributors are busy with other priority work and demands. Everyone's calendar is stacked with scheduled meetings. Individual personal calendars never match up to get the right people together for decision-making or problem-solving. For project teams, this is of particular concern, as delays in getting the right people together can impact the team's ability to meet deliverables on deadline.

An Alpha Meeting is a corporate method used to quickly convene ad hoc groups of staff from different parts of the company who would not ordinarily spend time together. Companies rely on Alpha Meetings to either define and/or resolve an urgent problem, or to make a decision that keeps a major project on track. At HPHC, if you are invited to an Alpha Meeting, attendance is mandatory. Two blocks of time are routinely reserved for these sessions: Mondays between noon and 2 p.m. and Wednesdays between 1 and 5 p.m. This means other standing meetings should avoid these times in order to minimize the potential for eventual disruption of previously scheduled activities. A project's executive sponsor, its project leader or project manager, can call an Alpha Meeting. The Project Management Office helps the organization avoid collisions by coordinating the Alpha scheduling. This practice has evolved over time; Alpha meeting space is available to any business leader who meets the urgent need to gather the "right" people quickly.

Project Status Meetings

Establishing standards for status meetings enables efficient transfer of information and documentation for priority projects. Here are five standard elements for project status meetings:

- **Attendees:** You must have a minimal number of participants to make the meeting valuable. If only you and one other participant arrive, you are probably wasting time. Be sure to set expectations regarding status meeting participation to avoid wasting time. At the very least, you should require your core team to participate. These are the critical members of your project team—the ones who are accountable for the project's success and hold the highest level of dependency. Participants should be members of your project team who can best speak to the project's progress, and who can relate risk and be accountable for actions.

- **Timing:** Weekly status meetings are the norm at HPHC. This frequency may increase to daily, depending upon the phase of the project and the number of critical issues to resolve. Seldom do HPHC project teams hold status meetings longer than a week apart—their projects have become increasingly more complex, representing an ongoing need for regular status updates. Establish a set time for each weekly meeting. People are more apt to attend when they know the status meeting is every Wednesday at 2 p.m., for example.

- **Duration:** A status meeting that lasts more than an hour is inefficient. A status meeting is designed to focus on project activities. If major issues or risks are identified, it is important to document them and determine next steps, due dates, and owners. Nothing is worse than inviting a core team to a status meeting, only to allow one member to speak. If more time is needed for regular status meetings, consider breaking the meeting into multiple sessions, with a specific focus on specific status updates.

- **Method:** As previously discussed, face-to-face interaction is most desirable. Since this is not always possible, run your meetings in a standard format, so everyone, regardless of where they are when they participate, will know what is expected of them during a status meeting.

- **Tools:** Project schedules, risk grids, and issues logs will help you run efficient meetings.

A Word on Virtual Meetings

Today, the global economy requires meetings with participants who are spread out across the country or around the world, raising new challenges for running successful meetings.

Facilitating a meeting face-to-face is still preferred, yet today it is not uncommon to run a meeting via phone, videoconferencing, or some alternate mode of communication. The way we work represents new challenges when we cannot have all participants together in one physical location. For example, today HPHC has multiple office locations, with staff working from regional locations across three New England states. They work with many vendors who are located in other regions of the country, and they have a number of staff people who work from home.

Be considerate and understanding of time differences. If you are inviting people who live in different time zones, go out of your way to identify a regular time that works for everyone. Be conscious of the time zone issue; do not operate and communicate only according to your own time zone. The act of recognizing other time zones will go a long way in building good will with your other participants.

Often, running a virtual meeting forces you to be efficient. You will be more conscientious about running the meeting according to schedule. However, the need to be efficient is apt to remove some of the intimacy created when everyone is meeting at the same location. Be sure to take the time to get to know your virtual team members and use this knowledge to add intimacy to the meeting, just as you would when running a local meeting. It's fine to share small chitchat with those team members who join the call early or first. (This, by the way, highlights the need for you, as the meeting leader, to always arrive on the call early, so you can assume the role of host.)

When conducting a virtual meeting, a little courtesy goes a long way. Be sure to know who is participating; welcome each joiner with a welcome and acknowledge their presence; this can be done by simply asking, "Who just joined us?" each time someone new jumps on. Use visual imagery; comments such as "I can sense you smiling" include participants as if everyone were in the same location.

Small actions can make a big difference. For example, if you are responsible for running virtual meetings, be sure you have the right equipment. Do not rely on speakerphones, for example, as you will lose credibility when it sounds like you are speaking from inside a tin can. Today, there are a number of high-tech gadgets to support conference call activities; equipment and options range from "spider" phones to dial-in conference call numbers. Both are good alternatives to support participants based in multiple locations. Know where the mute button is on your phone—nothing is worse than a few extra seconds of dead silence as you frantically search to release the mute button. Be careful, as you are apt to push the wrong button when under duress. A meeting leader will lose control if she disconnects in error. And always have contingency plans in place—what happens if the audio portion of the meeting goes down? If the call is disconnected or technology fails, who re-initiates the call? Simple rules should be determined before virtual meetings are established.

Defining Stakeholder Roles and Responsibilities

As mentioned earlier, having defined key stakeholder roles and responsibilities does not always determine project or team success. (In this example, stakeholders are those who have an impact on or are impacted by a project.) The key to success is the act of defining and communicating roles, so no one is confused or bewildered if roles are unfulfilled or expectations are not met. HPHC has standard definitions for project stakeholders; they are to be used as guidelines only, as each project team must assess their project individually to determine if the roles require adjustment. The three key roles include: Executive Sponsor, Project Lead and Project Manager.

Executive Sponsor
- Authorizes the project
- High-level business leader
- Provides leadership and vision
- Approves and signs scope document
- Removes corporate barriers to success
- Makes strategy decisions
- Communicates (generates enthusiasm)

Project Lead
- Appoints project manager
- Approves scope document
- Approves project plan
- Approves material changes (scope, cost, schedule)
- Resolves business issues and conflicts

[Note: The division of responsibility between Executive Sponsor and Project Lead may vary from project to project. The roles may also need to work hierarchically, depending upon organizational culture.]

Project Manager
- With project team, Executive Sponsor and Project Lead, finalizes project documentation
- Acts as the central contact point for all project team members
- Manages issues and sees that issues are resolved
- Facilitates communication within a project, and between project team and stakeholders
- Regularly briefs Executive Sponsor and Project Lead on project progress
- Manages resources, schedule, and scope change requests
- Completes weekly project status reports

Hub and Spoke

Ownership and accountability are key aspects of ensuring project success. Creating an infrastructure that involves the key project stakeholders is critical to monitoring project activities, identifying project risks, and promoting good communication among key players. A "Hub and Spoke" model coordinates activity among all necessary parties, supports rapid dissemination of information, and establishes a forum for fast issue resolution. This model is ideal for organizations introducing a project management methodology; it gathers project stakeholders on a regular basis to ensure projects are being managed according to methodology. For organizations with a mature methodology in place, it is an effective structure for promoting rapid resolution of priority projects, particularly projects with strong interdependent relationships. The PMO acts as the hub; representatives from key business units and projects act as the spokes, representing their respective areas.

Milestone Options

After a period of time, organizations can identify key characteristics of like projects. For example, product development initiatives and software development projects include predictable milestones. Once a PMO can easily identify typical milestones for similar projects, it can support project managers by offering typical milestone options for these initiatives. At HPHC, project managers can select typical milestones offered through drop-down menus for easy selection. Milestone options help guide project managers when they are completing scope documents and project schedules.

Keeping Track of Project Documentation

Many organizations conducting project management activities have difficulty keeping track of key project records. For organizations that invest in enterprise portfolio management systems, the challenges associated with storing documentation become less cumbersome. However, for smaller companies that do not want to make such a large investment and for organizations looking to introduce project management, keeping track of project information can be daunting. Companies often make mistakes when version-control is not in place; many project managers will use old or outdated project management tools, resulting in repeated work.

Regardless of what system you employ to track project documentation, there is a minimal set of requirements for being effective:

Central Project Repositories: A central storage area (both for paper and digital/electronic files) allows easy access to, availability of, and security for all project documentation.

Naming Conventions: Design a system that is uncomplicated. Many tools at HPHC are date qualified, as they sort correctly when someone is trying to locate the most current version, i.e. T.15 [project name] PSR 2005.12.28

Use Change Control/Version Control: Establish rules regarding updating and communicating. Be sure to inform users when changes have been made to existing templates and documents.

Establish Ownership: Maintain control over project documents and tools by assigning accountability through editing rights ownership.

Rapid Response Team

Project portfolios are complex. Most organizations face significant risk of unforeseeable disruption to successful project launches, as a result of limited resources. In spite of thorough project planning and resource estimation, it is often difficult to anticipate resource collisions, particularly when staff is already over-committed. Enterprise resource management tools are effective, but often miss key opportunities to identify resource discord until the clash occurs. Since many resources are pulled between project work and operations, it is inevitable that resource crack-ups will occur.

Establish an infrastructure that can respond quickly to business-critical issues posing a risk to successful delivery of the business plan.

The team should consist of a group of senior leaders who can represent the various business units throughout the organization and who should only deal with enterprise-wide issues that affect global resource contention and/or business collisions.

The PMO is the conduit for the group. It identifies enterprise-wide resource issues, as indicated by project resource management tools and by working with project leaders and business stakeholders. As soon as resource issues surface, the PMO alerts the group and asks it to function as an enterprise-wide forum providing rapid response to issues critical to the business plan. The group may be forced to solve resource issues that are obstacles to achieving business plan success. Here are a few examples of what the team may contend with:

- The organization does not have enough subject matter experts in a particular business to meet all project requirements; what does the team need to do to ensure all needs are met? Should resources be re-allocated? Should project deliverables and/or due dates be modified? Will redeployment of resources impact performance metrics?

- A major dependency between two projects has been identified, yet slipping deadlines on one project will negatively impact the dependent project; what needs to be done to ensure success? Do more resources need to be added to the project in trouble?

To be effective, the Rapid Response Team strives for a 24-hour turnaround on all decisions and/or recommendations. This team has the ability to make decisions for resource allocation within and across their respective business areas, as represented through the team membership. The team will seek executive decision on recommendations that impact adjustments to the business plan (i.e., stop, change, or move business plan components), budget, and performance metrics.

PMO Customer Satisfaction Survey

Much effort is required to develop a fully integrated EPMO in any organization. A sure way to assess progress is through administration of a customer satisfaction survey. The survey should be conducted annually and be sent to all constituencies who rely on or conduct project management activities. The survey should be designed to evaluate all services the PMO offers. Ideally, it should also solicit ideas and suggestions from staff regarding future improvements or enhancements. At HPHC, the annual survey evaluates the following areas:

- Responsiveness of PMO staff
- Availability and access to PMO
- Project management tools
- Project management consultation and assistance
- Meeting facilitation
- Executive reporting
- Project management-related training
- Business plan communications
- Direct management of projects
- PMPL sessions
- Project review process

The survey tool is designed with a 10-point scale in order to provide detailed feedback to the EPMO. There is also space for respondents to record comments, which further indicate the PMO performance. The results of the annual survey set improvement targets for the EPMO; much of the feedback is used to create the annual EPMO business plan.

Lesson of Threes
There is something about the number three. For example, a triangle is the most durable shape possible, the only "perfect" figure that, if all endpoints have hinges, will never change its shape unless the sides themselves are bent. Counting to three is common in situations where a group of people wish to perform an action in synchrony. The phrase "third time's a charm" usually means that the third time a person attempts something, he or she will succeed.

Likewise, when you are managing projects, the number three may mean something—good or bad—when you hear about an idea or an issue. If the topic comes up once, it may be simply interesting. If it comes up twice, it suggests, "pay attention." But hearing something stated three times, by different sources, usually represents Truth—it means action is required, or it is a fact.

HPHC's EPMO is sensitive to hearing issues repeat themselves, especially when they relate to project activities. For example, if three different parties that suggest how to implement a project make a similar suggestion three different times, HPHC takes heed of the information. If a situation happens in one meeting, it may not mean anything. If stated in two meetings, take notice. If the same issue is repeated at yet a third meeting, pursue it.

This philosophy can also apply during implementation. The first implementation is typically considered a pilot; the second iteration usually represents some improvement from the first; the third implementation effort almost always represents success. Pay attention to the Lesson of Threes.

It takes time to identify "best practices" in any organization. The EPMO is often the best judge of such practices and the most logical choice to spread the word about techniques offering the greatest results. Healthy team dynamics are equally important to project success, as no project can succeed without a project team. Chapter 8 explores ways to support good teamwork that leads to improved decisions, efficiency, and business results.

BUILDING REAL TEAMS

Talent wins games, but teamwork and intelligence wins championships.

Michael Jordan

No project can succeed without the efforts of a project team. In today's competitive environment, projects require a number of participants from different areas of an organization. Parties from external agencies will also likely be involved, whether they are consultants or vendors. Regardless of who is on a project team and how many members it has, the project will not meet deliverables and deadlines unless the group acts as a high-functioning team.

Creating Expected Behaviors

In 2002, Harvard Pilgrim CEO Charlie Baker recommended a set of expected behaviors for management and staff. This was right around the time the dust had begun to settle after the turnaround. Up until this point, Baker hadn't spent any time at all thinking about appropriate standards of behavior—nor had he ever said anything to anyone about how he thought standards should be developed or structured. "I had enough experience and had read enough books to know that after the turnaround, people were no longer brought together to simply help the company survive. There needed to be rules of engagement, and they needed to be explicit."

The behaviors were designed according to Baker's own views about what constituted appropriate behavior and strong leadership. They are intended to help facilitate the cross-functional teamwork that is critical to HPHC's success. The behaviors were further defined by a subset of senior managers selected to participate based upon their previous exhibition of teamwork characteristics. Participants included senior managers who exhibited "good" as well as "poor" team behaviors.

Determining the "right" set of behaviors to support productive teamwork is never easy, as team dynamics are intricate and difficult. Defining a set of behaviors to best support teamwork must be articulated in a universal language, because these behaviors need to be owned by the entire organization, not just upper management. At HPHC, the introduction of expected behaviors set the framework for ensuring these behaviors were a means of conducting business at Harvard Pilgrim Health Care.

To successfully define team behaviors, create a set of expected behaviors that use simple language, apply to organizational culture, and can be easily understood and practiced. No matter how large or small the organization, all expected behaviors must be clear and comprehensible to all staff, regardless of position or title. Organizations are more likely to realize results if they establish straightforward behaviors directly related to improving team dynamics. Create measurable behaviors so that staff can easily be held accountable.

When HPHC launched expected behaviors, Charlie Baker explained, "One of the items I've been telling people will be part of how we think about performance…is a set of 'expected behaviors.' These came out of conversations we've been having for the past few months about how important is it for everyone to think about this organization as a 'team' effort. There is no 'I' in HPHC. That said, here are the expected behaviors that we plan to incorporate into everyone's performance planning. You should view them as corporate standards for everyone."

HPHC Expected Behaviors

- Treat others with dignity and respect
- Support and promote intra- and inter-departmental teamwork
- Understand and consider the needs and impacts of your own work on others

118   *Simple Solutions*

- Demonstrate an ability to problem-solve and make timely decisions
- Actively seek and receive feedback for improvement
- Consistently share knowledge and information

Once behaviors are defined, it is important to construct a comprehensive communications plan to implement the behaviors across the organization and to promote their adoption. It took HPHC over two years to introduce and reinforce the Expected Behaviors program company-wide. The primary goal of the communications plan was to publicly promote Expected Behaviors to all staff, so all employees had a general understanding of the behaviors and heightened awareness of same during team interactions. During this initial two-year period, the senior management team continued to dedicate time to improving its own team dynamics. Senior management buy-in and endorsement is what makes team behavior work in an organization. Credible endorsement relies upon sincere actions; believable actions can occur only if senior leaders live the behaviors. This is often easier said than done.

Obtaining senior leadership buy-in is difficult because it requires numerous sessions and long hours dissecting and defining the expected behaviors. The behaviors themselves are not usually the issue—how leadership interprets and actually exhibits these behaviors is the challenge. There tends to be a natural split into three groups: Some senior leaders instinctively "get it"—they naturally exhibit positive team behaviors; others believe they practice the expected behaviors but are actually off the mark, as observed by their peers. The third segment simply denies the importance of the behaviors, doesn't exhibit the behaviors, and doesn't care.

At HPHC, the ones who "got it" were selected as cheerleaders to regularly promote the behaviors to their peers. The group who thought they got it but didn't exhibit the behaviors was given selective guidance through mentor relationships with other senior leaders. And the third segment received intensive one-on-one sessions, provided by outside experts. These sessions varied in duration and were provided based upon need. The intent of the coaching sessions was not to change someone's innate character but to enhance leadership capabilities through behavioral development. As HPHC expected, this continues to be an ongoing challenge for some people. Senior leaders must reach a level-based foundation, whereby members collectively exhibit effective Expected Behaviors, further enhancing productivity and efficiency. Once a minimal threshold is achieved, senior leaders are then able to lead the organization through example.

In 2004, Harvard Pilgrim made the management of group dynamics—and group project work—a major piece of their corporate agenda. HPHC launched Expected Behaviors in a more formal fashion by projectizing the effort. The idea was simple: HPHC does much of their work through groups; groups tend to be complex challenges from a management and communications point of view; and if they could come up with some ways to improve group dynamics, they could enhance group performance.

In recognition of the value of cross-functional teamwork, Harvard Pilgrim reinforced the set of Expected Behaviors to guide "how" they operate and achieve results through teams. The project goal was "to create an infrastructure for both the awareness and accountability for expected behaviors that is adopted and practiced throughout the organization, resulting in improved decisions, efficiency, and business results."

The scope of the initiative was set in phases. In 2004, HPHC introduced performance management activities in support of Expected Behaviors to all management staff. During the annual performance cycle, mid- to upper managers were given the opportunity to give and receive feedback relative to HPHC's Expected Behaviors. On a scale of 1 to 5, management staff was rated by their peers, supervisors, and teammates on each of the Expected Behaviors. It was a good way to build staff awareness of their behaviors and identify areas of strengths and weaknesses for each behavior. The feedback was used to develop staff performance plans.

HPHC's feedback form looks something like this:

Harvard Pilgrim
Health Care   *Expected Behavior Feedback Form*

1. HPHC Expected Behaviors

Based on your observation of this employee, use the scale below to rate the use of each Expected Behavior and provide specific behavioral examples:

Rating Scale—Models the Use of Expected Behaviors
0—Unknown
1—Strongly Disagree
2—Disagree
3—Neither Disagree nor Agree
4—Agree
5—Strongly Agree

Expected Behavior	0	1	2	3	4	5
Treat others with respect and dignity Comments/Examples of behavior:						
Support and promote intra- and inter-departmental teamwork Comments/Examples of behavior:						
Understand and consider needs and impacts of own work on others Comments/Examples of behavior:						
Solve problems and make timely decisions Comments/Examples of behavior:						
Actively seek and receive feedback for improvement Comments/Examples of behavior:						
Consistently share knowledge and information Comments/Examples of behavior:						

HPHC expanded the feedback process to all staff in 2005. Beginning in 2007, project team members are now evaluated within 30 days of project closure. This process allows project teams to evaluate one another, in real time, rather than wait until the end of the calendar year. This provides project-related feedback while the experience is still fresh. Project team members are now evaluated on both project delivery and Expected Behaviors. The idea is to present performance feedback to project team members before they are assigned to their next project. The goal is to give staff the opportunity to take the feedback to heart before their next project experience, so opportunities for improvement are realistically set.

Giving and receiving feedback is not a comfortable practice for most people. Feedback is often submitted anonymously, and frequently does not have documentation to support the ratings. Without specific examples, the receiver of the information is at a disadvantage—real examples provide information that is actionable. HPHC has found that practice makes better; the more often the feedback process occurs, the more comfortable staff become in both giving and receiving feedback. Based upon this observation, HPHC strongly encourages the exchange of feedback on a more frequent basis. A mid-year check is highly recommended; quarterly review of performance plans, including expected behavior feedback, is strongly encouraged.

Soliciting feedback does not need to be complex. In fact, the simpler, the better. People are busy with their own work and daily stresses; asking them to take the time to provide feedback on their co-workers takes some cajoling. The incentive appeals to people's self-interest: if you want feedback on yourself, be willing to provide it for others.

HPHC developed tools and rules of the road for managing group work and group communications around a simple concept: better communication and better group dynamics lead to higher performance, better decision-making, and improved project and business results. It also makes for a more productive and comfortable group working experience.

HPHC tested their Expected Behaviors tool kit with select teams for one year. Concentrating on project teams and other cross-functional business committees, HPHC introduced the Expected Behaviors Tool

Kit, focusing on key tools and their application in situations where behaviors were not being recognized or practiced. They trained participants through a multi-channel approach that included tool presentation and information via classroom-style and live vignettes demonstrating real behaviors. They leveraged online surveys to allow for immediate feedback and results.

Do's and Don'ts

HPHC knew creating a set of expected behaviors would set the foundation for achieving better business outcomes. (Meeting more project deliverables on time, for example.) Leaders also knew that staff would buy in to a simple set of behaviors only if they really understood the behaviors. Alan Slobodnik, co-founder and principal of Options for Change, assisted HPHC with the development of the "Do's and Don'ts." Alan is a senior consultant, trainer, and coach who specializes in organizational change; his practical method for intervening in human systems on the behavioral level guided HPHC through the identification of its Expected Behaviors.

Slobodnik believes successful organizations must invest time and energy to bring about true changes in behavior. "Many companies have core value statements posted on the wall. Harvard Pilgrim has gone the extra mile to ensure that the Expected Behaviors are both reflective of their culture and deeply embedded in it. Their commitment extends from rolling them out as an official corporate project, requiring their use on project teams and corporate committees, to embedding them in their HR systems." This, according to Slobodnik, is the best way to realize global acceptance and practice.

A subset of "Do's" and "Don'ts" was developed, where examples of good and bad behaviors articulate each Expected Behavior. The "Do's" and "Don'ts" list allows HPHC to correlate each Expected Behavior with suggested sample behaviors that general audiences could relate to on a day-to-day basis.

Expected Behaviors

DO	DON'T
Treat others with dignity and respect	
• Treat others as you would want to be treated.	• *Be a Bully* "Just do what I say!"
• Value the time and needs of others— e.g., start and end meetings on time; respond to all requests within 24 hours.	• *Be a Prima Donna* "I'll do this when I am good and ready."
• Recognize the value of others' views and perspectives.	• *Point the Finger* "That's the kind of thinking that created this problem."
• Support participation in problem-solving or decision-making discussions.	• *Be a Blowhard* "Why don't others speak up?"
Support and promote intra- and inter-departmental teamwork	
• Solve corporate, not just departmental problems.	• *Lose the Forest for the Trees* "All that really matters is that I get *my* job done."
• Play for the name on the front of the jersey by focusing on team rather than individual success.	• *Play for the Name on the Back of the Jersey.* "I've got to find a way to make sure I look good."
• Learn to involve your staff, your peers, and your boss in everything you do.	• *Play it Solo* "If I just work hard enough I can figure out and manage everything myself."

DO	DON'T
• Define the rules of the road and the rules of engagement: make sure roles are properly defined and assigned; establish service level agreements.	• *Drive Blind* "I have no idea what I'm supposed to be doing here or where this is going, but I'll go along for the ride."
• Understand that teamwork requires constructive role-playing.	• *Be a Ball Hog* "The only way we are going to score is if I shoot."
Understand and consider the needs and impacts of your own work on others	
• Understand that your work is part of a process and that your actions affect the work of others.	• *Work in a Silo* "I don't care how much work or disruption this causes for someone else."
• Acknowledge intersections and boundaries.	• *Eat Someone Else's Lunch* "I'll take credit for that, too, thanks!"
• Be open to different problem-solving approaches and solutions.	• *Be a Control Freak* "My totally closed mind is open to your proposal."
Demonstrate an ability to problem-solve and make timely decisions	
• Remember that problem-solving requires compromise; support decisions once they are made.	• *Sit in the Middle of the Road (and Cry)* "I don't like the solution so I am going to just sit here and make it hard for them to move."
• Behave in a professional, not personal, manner.	• *Wave the Red Cape* "This will really get Artie going."

DO	DON'T
• Be pro-ACT-ive.	• *Chase Rainbows* "If we just had perfect data, I would feel comfortable making a decision."
• Stay focused on the problem at hand and the time frame for resolution.	• *Shadow Box* "I know this has nothing to do with solving the problem, but I just love a good debate!"
• Identify and confront problems, no matter how big or ugly they may be.	• *Ignore the Rhino* "If we pretend there is no problem, maybe it will disappear."
Actively seek and receive feedback for improvement	
• Seek timely, frequent feedback from all internal customers.	• *Assume No News is Good News* "No one is saying anything bad; things must be good!"
• Listen actively and test your understanding.	• *Nod and Bob* "If I keep smiling, maybe they will believe I'm listening."
• Encourage both positive and negative feedback.	• *Go for the Jugular* "If you think I have a problem, you …"
Consistently share knowledge and information	
• Provide information in advance of meetings, with sufficient time for review.	• *Blindside* "If I don't tell them until I have to, I'll win."
• Share information with business partners.	• *Play Favorites* "Only my friends should know."

DO	DON'T
• Communicate information without bias or unwarranted conclusions.	• *Spin the Data* "I know I can make this data say what I think is true."
• Explain complicated information.	• *Drown with Paper* "They'll never understand this!"

The "Do's" and "Don'ts" were introduced to staff during the 2004 all-employee event. Staff watched senior leaders model behaviors, both good and bad, in a performance. Audience members quickly got it— they recognized the "Do's" and "Don'ts" in no time. They thoroughly enjoyed watching senior leaders poke fun at themselves through public displays of all kinds of behaviors.

The Tool Kit

As part of the plan to integrate these behaviors into how HPHC does business and manages projects, the company developed a Tool Kit using a combination of HPHC best practice tools and a select group of Options for Change FasTeams® Team Leadership Tools (already a part of HPHC's management development program). The kit contains simple user-friendly tools that teams can use to develop and refine their adoption of the Expected Behaviors.

A tool kit should include enough tools to meet team needs, but not so many tools that it overwhelms the users. HPHC placed sample tools for each Expected Behavior in the tool kit, for a total of sixteen tools. They don't expect or require project teams to go through the entire Tool Kit or to use all the tools. Some are designed to help teams initially agree on how they will operate, and are only revisited if those agreements are not being kept. Others are included for the purpose of helping teams address specific problems caused by not practicing a given Expected Behavior. Overall, the Tool Kit is used to encourage the healthy differences of opinion that naturally arise and enable the kind of respectful debate that occurs all the time in high-performing teams.

HPHC's experience to date suggests one size does not fit all. They know that minimum conditions of success include leadership buy-in, stable team membership, and a commitment to purpose. Success also relies on early engagement. Project teams that introduce Expected Behaviors early in team development are more successful. Success comes when teams use a couple of quick and simple tools, are not overly prescriptive in their approach, and have mentors available to them as needed.

Walking the Talk

To ensure both awareness and accountability, all project teams responsible for a corporate-level project are required to adhere to these behaviors by progressing through a series of stage-gate activities in support of Expected Behaviors. Project teams are required to participate in a minimal set of activities and tool use; the requirements were defined by what worked well for other teams during the pilot phase. The PMO liaisons act as Expected Behavior coaches to project teams, further promoting project success by supporting team dynamics. Expanding the PMO liaison's purview to include team dynamics was a natural evolution of the PMO liaison role. The expanded role better supports project teams as they manage complex projects, by offering both technical and "soft" skill consultation. This is another example of where the EPMO, through evolution, continues to offer value to HPHC as a whole.

The required set of activities includes a structured team conversation on Expected Behaviors, the completion of an Expected Behaviors Survey, a Rules of Engagement exercise, and use of standard meeting management templates.

Expected Behaviors Discussion Guide

The Discussion Guide was developed to assist team leaders (project managers) in planning a discussion with their team about the impact and value of adopting Expected Behaviors as a way to enhance team effectiveness. The intent is to have the project manager initiate a discussion that guides the team to evaluate which behaviors are done well and identify where and how improvements could be made.

Engaging team members in this discussion is not as difficult as you might expect. The key to having a successful dialogue is timing—when to have such a conversation defines success more often than the actual exchange itself. Timing is critical. Teams should not conduct this discussion too early; a group needs some time to cohere as a team before being able to evaluate its ability to behave well. On the other hand, don't wait too long, because bad behavior is hard to change. HPHC's experience suggests a successful dialogue for project teams occurs during the first three months of team formation. This obviously needs to be adjusted for teams with abbreviated project start/end dates.

The project manager (team leader) starts the discussion by setting the context. It is important to reinforce the value of team behaviors from the leader's perspective. The leader should express personal commitment to team behaviors and acknowledge that even leaders don't always get them "right." As such, the leader must give the team permission to hold each other accountable, including the leader. The team leader must actively seek input from each team member as to whether the leader is demonstrating Expected Behaviors. Sharing the idea that all team members must hold each other accountable to demonstrate these behaviors is critical.

Have team members assess their team's current adherence to Expected Behaviors. This can be done in a number of ways. For HPHC, the easiest and most successful way to collect this feedback is by survey. All team members are asked to take an Expected Behaviors Survey, which is a simple way to measure adherence to HPHC's Expected Behaviors. The survey looks like this.

Expected Behavior Survey

Based on your experience to date, we are interested in knowing how strong you believe the "PMO Team" is in the following areas.
Using a scale of 1-7, where 1 = extremely weak, and 7 = extremely strong, please rate the following:

1. Members consistently treat each other with dignity and respect.

Extremely Weak   1   2   3   4   5   6   7   Extremely Strong

              O   O   O   O   O   O   O

2. Members support and promote intra- and inter- departmental teamwork.

Extremely Weak   1   2   3   4   5   6   7   Extremely Strong

              O   O   O   O   O   O   O

3. Team/Members are sensitive to how their needs, ideas, or suggestions will impact the workload of others on the team.

Extremely Weak   1   2   3   4   5   6   7   Extremely Strong

              O   O   O   O   O   O   O

4. Team/Members are sensitive to how their needs, ideas, or suggestions will impact the workload of others not on the team.

Extremely Weak   1   2   3   4   5   6   7   Extremely Strong
     O O O O O O O

5. Members effectively work together at problem resolution.

Extremely Weak   1   2   3   4   5   6   7   Extremely Strong
     O O O O O O O

6. Team is effective in making timely decisions.

Extremely Weak   1   2   3   4   5   6   7   Extremely Strong
     O O O O O O O

**7. Members actively seek out opinions
and feedback from each other.**

Extremely Weak   1   2   3   4   5   6   7   Extremely Strong
     O O O O O O O

8. Members discuss ideas and suggestions on how to improve.

Extremely Weak   1   2   3   4   5   6   7   Extremely Strong
              O   O   O   O   O   O   O

**9. Members consistently share knowledge
and information with each other.**

Extremely Weak   1   2   3   4   5   6   7   Extremely Strong
              O   O   O   O   O   O   O

Once the survey results are in, there are a number of questions the team can use to initiate the team discussion:

- Do Expected Behaviors impact our group's Effectiveness? If so, how?
- Survey data shows that we do this Expected Behavior well, what does performing "well" look like?
- Even if we perform an Expected Behavior well, should we try to raise the bar? If so, how?
- Which Expected Behaviors need improvement?
- What does it look like when we don't perform this Expected Behavior well?
- What needs to happen to make it "safe" to give feedback to each other?
- How will we communicate to each other if an Expected Behavior is not being practiced?

- Why should we make the effort to change our own behavior related to this Expected Behavior? What's in it for us?
- How will we know when we are successfully practicing this Expected Behavior?
- Are we willing to try using a support tool to help us improve our use of an Expected Behavior?
- How and when will we evaluate the usefulness of the tool?
- If another team that we interact with violates the Expected Behavior, how should this be handled?

The results of the team's discussion will determine next steps. If a team has much opportunity for improvement, the team leader must work with the team to prioritize areas of pain. The best way to realize success is through team engagement.

The survey is a good way to obtain a baseline measurement of the team's ability to work well together. Because the survey is done anonymously, participants are more inclined to answer honestly. Once a team has baseline results, it is ready to acknowledge strengths and tackle areas where improvement is needed. The survey is also a great way to track and record a team's progress over time. Teams should wait six months to one year before taking a second survey. Project teams have constraints around this; if a project team is in place for less than six months, there really isn't time to conduct a follow-up survey. This model works very well for long-term teams, as it provides a chrono-logical view of team growth and development. Because long-standing teams will sometimes experience degradation in results, this survey is a great way to catch early warning signals.

Rules of Engagement

Conducting a Rules of Engagement conversation will allow team members to develop an initial contract that describes how they will treat each other with dignity and respect. Since the meaning of "treating others with dignity and respect" varies from individual to individual, this tool will help the team identify and discuss the various elements of behavior that are critical to the success of ongoing interactions. The Rules of Engagement exercise focuses on six key areas of behavior:

- Basic Courtesies
- Operating Agreement
- Problem-Solving and Decision-Making
- Accountability
- Conflict Resolution
- Leader's Role

In a team meeting, schedule extra time to focus on this. If a team does not dedicate time to this exercise, it will never happen. Many HPHC teams schedule a special session dedicated solely to Rules of Engagement. In this meeting, team members brainstorm and record a list of key behaviors that are important to them and that best support operating agreements. They use the "Do's and Don'ts" as a jumping-off point. Consider asking such questions as, *How do you like to work? What is your work style? What strengths do you bring?* Allow time for discussion of the key areas and behaviors that the team wants to adopt. Ensure all voices are heard.

Run through each of the six key areas; all are important. However, teams may find that not all have equal weight. For example, Conflict Resolution may be more important to the group than Operating Agreement. Focus on getting through all areas while seeking common ground for consensus. Be sure to confirm that each area is complete before moving on. A team leader may need to solicit input from quiet team members; not everyone will have the same voice. As facilitators, it is important that team leaders acknowledge others' contributions to the discussion before relating their own remarks. Never distort others' views in order to advance your own. To be successful, the results of this exercise must represent the team's collective input. It is not unusual for the PMO Liaison to facilitate this discussion; having a non-biased, unattached person lead the Rules of Engagement discussion often frees participants to share opinions.

Once the group decides on the key areas of behavior, they document and post their Rules of Engagement at every meeting as a reminder. Depending upon the duration of the team, the group can decide if the agreement needs to be refreshed; often teams do not return to their agreement unless there are challenges in a particular area.

The results of a Rules of Engagement exercise should produce a team charter that looks something like this:

Rules of Engagement Worksheet **Treat others with dignity & respect**

Basic Courtesies

- Limit Blackberry use to check on ONLY urgent or emergency messages; if an urgent message requires an urgent response, leave the room to respond.
- Don't interrupt until the person speaking finishes.
- Listen to and respect the viewpoint of others.
- Arrive on time for the meeting.
- No sidebar conversations.

Operating Agreements

- Create team meeting calendar to ensure schedule of work is clear and that we cover all aspects of that work.
- Distribute agendas and supporting materials two days in advance.
- Post all materials to project team database.
- Meetings will begin at 1:05 PM and conclude at 2:55 PM
- Start and end all meetings on time.
- Begin each meeting with a review of meeting minutes; minutes to include all decisions, with supporting rationale.

- Members should complete a meeting evaluation at the end of the last meeting of each month.

Problem-Solving and Decision-Making

- Make a decision based on what is reasonable from a business perspective and what will solve the problem, rather than hold out for perfection.
- Identify and confront problems. Focus on the issues, not the people.
- Focus on making the timeliest decision possible. If necessary, follow up on issues off-line.
- Make decisions based on presentation of a combination of facts, experience, and judgment.

Accountability

- Presenters need to ensure that presentations are clear and concise and address problem at hand.
- Each member needs to support the project manager by helping drive constructive conflict, and timely resolution of issues and decision-making.
- Project Manager holds self and others accountable.
- Take responsibility—no finger-pointing or blaming.

Conflict Resolution

- Make sure that we fully engage in the discussion.
- Make the conversation about the business problem and not people—don't hold back if conflict emerges.
- Ensure that discussion remains on point and that discussion does not become tangential to main topic.
- Ensure meeting is facilitated and keeps to agenda and schedule.

- If a conflict cannot be resolved within the meeting, the issue will be addressed off-line; an update will be shared with the group at a later time.
- On regular basis, review results of meeting evaluations. Address feedback proactively.

Leader's Role

- Take responsibility for task completion and accountability.
- Ensure presenters are well-prepared and on point.

(Note: The Rules of Engagement Tool is copyrighted material from Options for Change, to be used only with permission.)

Successful Facilitation

Project Managers sometimes find this Rules of Engagement exercise difficult. It requires facilitation skill, one of those "soft" skills not often taught in the project management world. To successfully facilitate this discussion, project managers must guide the group so all members of the team are engaged in the discussion and own the results. Project managers cannot force the team to accept the leader's desires; the results need to be fully owned by all team members in order to hold weight.

While facilitating, the team leader must listen carefully to others. Ask clarifying questions to further understand what someone is saying; it is better to ask than to interpret incorrectly. Remember that silence can speak volumes; allowing some space in between comments creates an opportunity for team members to digest what someone has said. This will allow others to add to the previous comment or offer a slightly different view. Creating silence is never easy, but is necessary to ensure full team collaboration. Here are some key phrases to help facilitate this exercise:

- "What I heard you say is…."
- "Can you give us an example so we can better understand what you are saying?"

- "Do we agree on this item?"
- "Does anyone have a different perspective to offer?"
- "Have we exhausted this topic? Are we ready to move on?"

For skeptics who perceive this activity as nonsense and a waste of time when there is constructive and important project work to deliver, keep this in mind: Teams who conduct this exercise indicate their teams are positively impacted by the experience. Communication and working relationships improve; team members become more aware of behaviors toward others, more aware of others' roles, and better at seeing different points of view. HPHC teams say the exercise creates a more comfortable working environment, meetings are more productive, and teams are more efficient in meeting deliverables. The big surprise for most team leaders is the realization that the activities are not time-consuming, do not slow down work, nor do they stifle team energy or limit lively and productive discussion.

The size of a project team will determine how you conduct this exercise. If a project manager is leading a large program, with hundreds of staff assigned, a Rules of Engagement exercise cannot be conducted in one sitting. At HPHC, the optimum crowd seems to be twenty participants. For larger programs, there are creative ways to conduct this exercise. A leader may want to conduct this with core leaders only. A team leader could develop a "trickle-down" system, whereby project managers assigned to each sub-team are responsible for leading their own discussions. Regardless of how a Rules of Engagement session is conducted, remember these two key points: A team must have total team engagement, and must document their results to be effective.

Case Study

The Vendor Fulfillment project was well underway when HPHC introduced Expected Behaviors, leaving too little time to measure effectiveness of the survey tool and Discussion Guide in any real way. Instead, the project core team met and reviewed the Expected Behaviors when they came out and conducted an abbreviated version of Rules of Engagement. Their Rules of Engagement were documented on a flip chart as a way to remind themselves of the importance of team dynamics.

Thrasivoulos has employed the Expected Behaviors tool kit on subsequent projects. He has found the Survey and Rules of Engagement tools to be the most effective. According to Thrasivoulos, the survey tool easily identifies team strengths and weaknesses; the Rules of Engagement exercise enables his project team(s) to flag and fix team behavior smoothly. Taken together, this is an effective preventive course of treatment for successful team dynamics.

Other Tools in the Box

There are a number of other tools in the Expected Behaviors toolbox. Each tool was designed to address key team development skills, such as problem solving and decision- making, negotiating and conflict resolution, giving and receiving feedback, stakeholder involvement, and communication. Each tool addresses common ailments found in teams. The tools are available on a self-treatment basis—teams are able to freely pick and choose as needed, and are also able to receive additional support through their Liaison, should they need further support and guidance while addressing a particularly painful team issue.

Standard Meeting Management Tools

HPHC created two tools for the Tool Kit as afterthoughts: Meeting Agenda and Meeting Minute templates. At first, HPHC did not believe it was necessary to include these tools, as they assumed all effective teams automatically use such tools on a day-to-day basis. After all, how does a team conduct a successful meeting without them? The tools are very simple, generic templates to support meeting management; HPHC simply added their Expected Behaviors to each tool. Much to their surprise, they found that many project teams had not been using meeting management tools on a regular basis. As such, the templates became very popular very quickly. Here is what they look like.

Harvard Pilgrim
HealthCare

Team or Project Name
Meeting Agenda
Date, Time, Location

Attendees:

Facilitators:

Goal:

Harvard Pilgrim Health Care Expected Behaviors	
Treat others with dignity and respect	Support and promote intra- and inter- departmental teamwork
Understand and consider the needs and impacts of your own work on others	Demonstrate an ability to problem-solve and make timely decisions
Actively seek and receive feedback for improvement	Consistently share knowledge and information

DURATION	AGENDA TOPIC	WHO	GOAL

Team or Project name
Meeting Minutes

Harvard Pilgrim Health Care Expected Behaviors	
Treat others with dignity and respect	Support and promote intra- and inter-departmental teamwork
Understand and consider the needs and impacts of your own work on others	Demonstrate an ability to problem-solve and make timely decisions
Actively seek and receive feed-back for improvement	Consistently share knowledge and information

Meeting Information

Date:	
Project/Team Name:	
Facilitator:	
Meeting Goal:	

Meeting Participants—Name, Title and Department
Tab inserts next row

1.
2.

Decisions *Tab inserts next row*

-
-

Open Action Items/Issues *Tab inserts next row*				
Open Action Items	Description	Owner	Date Due	Closed Date
1.				
2.				

Closed Action Items/Issues *Tab inserts next row*			
Closed Action Items	Description	Resolution	Completion Date
1.			

According to HPHC CEO Charlie Baker, the introduction of Expected Behaviors has made a difference. "People do know the difference between good and bad behavior, and while we still have bad behavior, people generally acknowledge it and try to correct it." He also thinks it has helped HPHC work cross-functionally. "It's not an objective that's ever completely achieved, but instead represents a way of measuring directional performance. And on that count, I do believe we get better, each year." You can't ask for more than that.

Workforce development must occur continuously across all levels of staff for organizations to succeed. Chapter 9 examines how establishing a project management career path can build and strengthen project management competencies within your organization.

CHAPTER 9

WHAT MAKES A GREAT
PROJECT MANAGER?

To succeed, one must possess an effective combination of ability, ambition, courage, drive, hard work, integrity, and loyalty.

Harry F. Banks

Establishing a Project Management Career Path

Project management has received increased recognition over recent years, as more and more businesses appreciate the benefits provided through project management skill and practice. Originally relegated to fields like engineering, aerospace, and construction, project management has expanded across virtually all industries, creating a need for "qualified" project managers.

Let's look at how the project management profession has exploded. The Project Management Institute (PMI) is a nonprofit, international organization that has provided decades of research, guidelines, and standards for the project management community. Five volunteers established PMI in 1969. The group offered its first PMI Seminar that year, which drew 83 attendees. Membership erupted in the mid-nineties, during the high-tech boom. As of 2006, the PMI community consisted of 220,000 members, with over 180,000 project management professionals (PMPs) in 175 countries.

Project management is shifting its focus; it is no longer just an execution model, it is also a strategic business model. Out of the organizations that already appreciate the value of project management in completing tasks, many have also recently begun to realize project management's critical contribution, from delivering completed projects to being strategic owners who deliver business value.

Yet, in spite of a growing project management presence, "accidental" project managers are still the norm, not the exception. Many companies continue to treat projects in a fairly unstructured manner and, as a result, do little to invest in their project managers. Many project managers have little authority or power in their role, and the majority of individuals who manage projects typically do so while juggling other job responsibilities.

Organizations must be prepared and willing to invest in project managers to fully realize the benefits of project management. There is no point in instituting a project management methodology without introducing a project management career path. Having one without the other will limit success.

So, why are organizations remiss in supporting the project management role? Many don't know how to describe a good project manager. It's true that a first-rate project manager sounds like a fantastical being—proficient at planning and problem-solving; adept at budgeting; an accomplished negotiator and master influencer who is able to lead, motivate, and communicate. Oh, and a first-rate project manager remains calm during the height of the storm. In other words, this is someone who must be able to handle it all. So many requirements, yet so few candidates. Organizations must be willing to define project manager requirements and invest in the project manager role to realize business success.

Until recently, HPHC was not unlike other organizations. In spite of having a strong project management methodology and an organizational belief in project management practice, HPHC did not have alignment of a structured project manager job "family" or clear requirements for such positions. HPHC lacked well-defined, consistent job descriptions and "clarity" around role definition in the organization. Current incumbents of project management-type positions at the same level were not consistent across the company in terms of job definition, responsibilities, levels, scope, and salary. This gap prevented HPHC from finding the "right" project managers to meet organizational requirements. It also failed to provide a clear and equitable career path for individuals who were currently performing project manager-like roles and who sought future growth and opportunity.

In 2003, HPHC embarked on a journey to establish a project management career path in the company. A partnership between HPHC's PMO and Human Resources (HR) departments was formed, and the work efforts were organized as a project. The project goal was to establish, implement, and properly slot incumbents into a structured project management job family that offered consistency throughout HPHC. The structure would allow for easy identification of project management resources as needed, retention of current incumbents, and recruitment of candidates with the right qualifications. It would also identify needed training and coaching for appropriate individuals.

The effort took over a year to complete. The challenges associated with introducing a project management career path are not unlike those associated with introducing a project management methodology: the technical aspects of the process must be balanced against the operational, cultural, and behavioral needs of each individual organization to work; functional barriers must be eliminated; communications need to be ever-present.

Deb Hicks (previously introduced in Chapter 4) knows efforts toward organizational success often require transparency between departments. Functional areas, including individual managers, must work together to address business needs. Working together to establish a project management career path is a perfect example of where an alliance across an organization will produce needed results. "Managers need to be willing to share strengths and development needs of staff who are assigned to corporate projects. This allows for an organizational approach to talent development. HR and the PMO departments also must utilize corporate systems, like the Performance Planning and Appraisal process, to drive development as well as accountability."

While there are industry standards that can easily be applied when establishing project manager roles, they should always be judged against an individual company's needs and values. The extended timeframe for completing the process at HPHC enabled proper allocation of HR support, consideration of critical initiatives (including reorganizations) in the business, and proper slotting of over 100 positions across the organization. The schedule also enabled considerable dialogue between HR, the PMO and the business during role definition, to ensure all considerations were made before and during implementation efforts.

How to Do It

When establishing a project management career path, keep the process simple and engage the business. Regardless of where project managers reside in your organization—centrally located within the PMO or distributed across the business—they all support business requirements. Be sure to solicit input from all key business stakeholders before introducing project manager roles, as all business leaders have a vested interest in project manager competency.

The process can be completed in six steps:

1. Review and evaluate position descriptions

2. Create project manager templates

3. Slot incumbents into appropriate positions

4. Create alternate titles for positions determined to be non-project management

5. Set up positions within HR/Payroll systems

6. Establish a system to periodically evaluate project manager positions

Let's look at these six steps individually.

1. How to Review and Evaluate

If your organization already has project manager roles and well-defined job descriptions, then this first step is simply a matter of periodically reviewing the descriptions to determine if they still apply, given business and industry needs. It's more likely, however, that the functions exist in the absence of accurate job descriptions. In this case, it is imperative to get feedback from major stakeholders (business owners who oversee project manager positions or business owners who reap the direct results of well-managed projects) during this process. It is also ideal to have a few "project managers" participate, as the function is apt to vary widely, particularly if project managers are spread across the organization.

An efficient way to seek feedback is through focus groups. Invite all key stakeholders to a session designed to solicit honest feedback in a safe environment. This may work best if it is conducted by a non-biased facilitator who is not connected to project management, the PMO, or the HR departments. However, it is important to have these individuals observe or attend the focus group session.

Present draft role descriptions; collect and synthesize feedback so common factors can be easily identified. Remember, the purpose of this exercise is to identify common-denominator elements in defining project manager functions. It is best to create foundational requirements associated with each role—detailed variations are best located in specific job descriptions, the next step after role descriptions.

Start the exercise by presenting draft descriptions to your stakeholder audience. Seek their reaction and comments. Ask them for specific examples to support their opinions. Remember, this process is highly iterative and often requires multiple sessions. Each round of feedback will modify the descriptions in some way; this is the best way to create accurate descriptions the business will readily understand and accept. This is also the most effective way to obtain business buy-in.

Be patient with the feedback you receive. Stakeholder reaction will be different if you are introducing project manager descriptions for the very first time rather than adjusting existing descriptions. Be sensitive to emotional reactions and the fear of change. If project managers reside in functional business units, be prepared for stakeholders to be protective of their staff; this protectiveness may cause participants to hold back in declaring the current role of their project managers, especially if there is any chance of structural changes. When HPHC launched activities to review and adjust project manager titles and job descriptions, business owners were informed from the start that the exercise would not result in organizational changes. HPHC was interested in assessing and defining true project manager positions; they were not interested in moving project managers out of, or between, functional units.

When HPHC conducted the feedback sessions, each session was well-documented; participant comments were recorded without debate, ownership, or emotion. Maintaining a focus on the business requirements will produce actionable feedback. Here are a few examples of the types of comments HPHC received during the feedback sessions, which supported further edits to the descriptions:

- "The template seems to have too much emphasis on time (90%) as opposed to skills and other (cross-functional) project expertise."

- "Demonstration of competency should be required at each level."

- "Redefine or set minimum budget oversight."

- "Anybody who works as a project manager less than 50% of the time should not have a project manager title, in fact project managers should work 100% of the time managing projects."

2. How to Create Them

Positions must have clear responsibilities, scope, and requirements, as well as career paths for each project manager title. Template descriptions should be created with standard headers. At HPHC, the leveled descriptions include the following areas:

- Responsibilities (summary of the position)

- Education (or equivalent)

- Experience

- Knowledge (breadth and depth)

- Soft skills required

- Responsibility for work of others

- Scope

- Reporting relationship

When creating the template document, it is wise to include all positions within the project manager family. This enables stakeholders to

easily see the differences across roles. At HPHC, there are four project
manager-related positions:

- Project Manager Administrator (PMA)
- Project Manager 1 (PM1)
- Project Manager 2 (PM2)
- Project Manager 3 (PM3)

Here is what HPHC's Project Manager Family Template structure
looks like today. Any organization can easily adapt the framework to
meet its own needs when defining a project management career path.

PROJECT MANAGER FAMILY TEMPLATE DESCRIPTIONS				
LEVEL	PMA	PM1	PM2	PM3
RESPONSIBILITIES **(summary of position)**				

PROJECT MANAGER TEMPLATE DESCRIPTIONS				
LEVEL	PMA	PM1	PM2	PM3
EDUCATION* *or equivalent*				
EXPERIENCE				

PROJECT MANAGER FAMILY TEMPLATE DESCRIPTIONS				
LEVEL	PMA	PM1	PM2	PM3
KNOWLEDGE Breadth/ Depth				

PROJECT MANAGER TEMPLATE DESCRIPTIONS				
LEVEL	PMA	PM1	PM2	PM3
Soft Skills required				

PROJECT MANAGER TEMPLATE DESCRIPTIONS				
LEVEL	PMA	PM1	PM2	PM3
RESPONSIBILITY FOR WORK OF OTHERS				
SCOPE				
TYPICALLY REPORTS TO				

Once again, this grid should be used as a guide only; every organization has differing needs and requirements; role descriptions do not come in a one-size-fits-all design.

3. The Challenge of Slotting

Placing staff into project manager roles can be the most difficult task associated with the process. The reason this is so difficult is that it relies on a level of subjective thinking. Creating descriptions that are crisp, with well-defined requirements, will reduce the level of subjectivity involved in the process.

To assist with the slotting process, HPHC created a Project Manager Self-Assessment tool. The optional self-assessment tool was designed to help supervisors and managers include "project managers" in the process, identify any discrepancies between what the job description states about positions and what the incumbents are actually doing. It is also a great way to initiate dialogue with incumbents about where they may fall within the new project manager framework. The tool was created in response to supervisor and manager requests—further supporting their role in this process. Information obtained through the self-assessment tool is kept between the supervisor and the incumbent; it is not shared with HR unless the supervisor seeks further guidance in evaluating an incumbent's appropriate level.

When creating a self-assessment tool, be sure to include elements that align with the template descriptions. At HPHC, the following areas were included:

- Profile of project work accomplishments
- Education
- Technical knowledge
- Experience
- Knowledge of project management areas
- Business process redesign
- Skills required for current projects being managed

- Further discussion: This includes other strengths, talents, or expertise; areas of development identified via tool completion; additional training received at HPHC which has strengthened project manager competencies

Harvard Pilgrim's HR and PMO staff provided support and consultation to the supervisors responsible for the slotting activities. PMO guidance focused on technical evaluation, industry knowledge, and an understanding and appreciation of the types of projects typically listed in the portfolio. HR advice primarily focused on training in communications skills for the managers responsible for having these discussions with incumbent project managers. For example, HPHC provided scripts to supervisory staff, to help guide the discussions.

4. Create Alternate Positions

This exercise not only allows for consistency across the project management profession, it also enables organizations to clean up outdated positions. The goal of the exercise is to slot all project managers into appropriately leveled positions and to create a career path for the project manager position. In some instances, you may find some incumbents fall outside the project manager family. This allows supervisors and HR to work together to identify a more appropriate title for these positions.

5. Set Up Systems

Once candidates are slotted in the appropriate roles, the organization must have the proper infrastructure to support the positions. All HR and payroll systems must be updated to include the new positions, so there is accurate end-to-end administration of the project manager roles within the organization (as well as for any other newly defined positions).

6. Conduct Reviews

Project manager positions must be reviewed and evaluated on a periodic basis in the same fashion that other positions are regularly appraised. To attract and retain top-notch project managers, organizations must invest time and effort in routinely evaluating positions. This includes market analysis, salary benchmarking, professional standards, and certification requirements. This periodic assessment relies on the continued partnership between the EPMO and HR departments.

The Final Ingredient

Once again, the final ingredient in the recipe is communication. A comprehensive communications plan must be developed to guide the organization through the process. Essential messaging, including "why, who, what, and when" must be provided, so all key stakeholders fully understand the work, the rationale behind the work, and the output of the work.

The Four E's

As we've emphasized throughout this book, project managers are expected to perform heroics to successfully execute a company's strategic plan. Individuals must be multi-faceted, have technical know-how, and exhibit strong leadership skills, just to name a few requirements. Regardless of the credentials a project manager holds, there are four primary characteristics every project manager must exhibit to be successful:

Enthusiasm: A successful project manager must really want to do the job. He or she must get intense enjoyment from leading a project. If a project manager is not enthusiastic about the project, it's really hard for other team members to get on board.

Endurance: Project management requires high levels of staying power. In the beginning everything is unclear—the project goal, the project schedule, the project team, the roles and responsibilities. A successful project manager must endure all stages of project management, from project definition through project execution to project closure. Getting through this phase will enable you to reach the next.

Earnest: Project managers must be sincere and serious in intention. Sincerity will enable project managers to establish a strong coalition among team members, while keeping focused on getting the work done. A team's ability to work together will get it through the tough spots.

Efficient: Project managers who work productively with minimum wasted effort and with limited resources will always succeed. The best project managers will keep an eye on the target and establish a direct route to get there.

What Does a Successful Project Manager Look Like?

Project managers come in all shapes and sizes, with varying levels of training, experience, education, and background. Some come with professional project management credentials, others do not. Some have spent their entire professional careers managing projects, while others have strong ambitions to become project managers. And there are many candidates who fall in between these extremes. The challenge for every organization is to know what you want in a project manager before you search for one. Be thoughtful and precise in assessing the level of project management proficiency you need (to support the size, type, and magnitude of your project portfolio) and overlay those requirements with emotional, social, and interpersonal intelligence requirements.

In fact, be careful not to over-emphasize technical requirements when evaluating candidates. Limiting your search to individuals who have strong technical abilities, but lack professional decorum and interpersonal skills is not likely to produce optimum results when managing projects. Hiring project managers who are proficient in technical application of project management practice, but lack patience, tolerance, and understanding are not likely to attain great success. Instead, they are more likely to alienate project sponsors and project team members. A project manager who can get the job done but leaves a trail of injured spirits in his or her path is a less-than-ideal candidate for any organization.

Only in the last five years have project managers been recognized as needing keen technical skills *and* top management skills to be effective. In fact, some believe grooming project managers with a 360-degree focus on all key leadership attributes is a successful recipe for creating future business leaders and CEOs. The challenge is this: project managers have been around for much longer than the past five years—so, how can you recognize a "good" one?

How to Select the "Right" Project Manager

Screening project manager candidates requires hiring managers to see beyond credentials and accomplishments. Traditional interview questions still apply when assessing project manager candidates. These questions typically include:

- Tell me about yourself.

- What are the roles and responsibilities in your current position?

- Whom do you report to?

- What size projects do you manage?

- What size is your project team(s)?

- What is the average length of your projects?

- Are you PMI-certified?

To see past a candidate's resume, take the time to fully evaluate the person thoroughly. Using behavior-based methods to screen candidates has become increasingly popular. The premise behind behavioral interviewing is that the most accurate predictor of future performance is past performance in similar situations. The key is delving deeply enough during the interview process to accurately assess past behavior. Behavioral interviewing requires the interviewer to ask questions in a way that reveals a candidate's true character. The interviewer must probe to reach a depth of details that forces candidates to share previous experiences and behaviors. Interviewers must ask pointed questions to elicit detailed responses that reveal whether the candidate possesses the desired characteristics.

Suppose, for example, an interviewer asks, "How would you handle XYZ situation?" The responder has minimal accountability. However, suppose the interviewer continues to probe by asking, "What were you thinking at that point?" or "Lead me through your decision process." This tactic is apt to provide far more insight about the candidate and his/her ability to handle tough situations. Continuous probing of a situation puts the pressure on; this also enables the interviewer to observe the candidate's ability to hold up under a barrage of difficult questions.

When you create a line of questions designed to uncover a candidate's true personality, you can discover "multiple intelligences" to determine if the candidate will fit the requirements of the position and your organization's culture. The phrase "emotional intelligence" was coined by Yale psychologist Peter Salovey and the University of New Hampshire's John Mayer to describe qualities like understanding one's own feelings, empathy for the feelings of others, and "the regulation of emotion in a way that enhances living." In October 1995, Nancy Gibbs wrote an article on emotional intelligence for *Time Magazine*, in which she suggests that a triumph of the reasoning brain over the impulsive one is emotional intelligence, and, regardless of one's cognitive ability (i.e., IQ), each of us has an emotional intelligence that natural talent seems to ignite in some people and dim in others.

In the area of emotion, the distinction between intelligence and knowledge is murky and debate continues today around our true ability to distinguish between the two. Yet, there is enough evidence to suggest that plenty of "smart" individuals have little understanding of their emotions and don't know how to use emotions in their communication and relationships. Conversely, there are many people who are "feelers," whose behavioral tendencies dismiss logic and rational approaches. Neither type of individual will succeed as a project manager unless they are able to find a balance.

Vicki Coates, Vice President, Benefits, Products & Market Performance at HPHC, applies this line of questioning when screening project manager candidates. Coates delves into a candidate's mind by asking questions about why he or she has been successful or what the person would have done differently. She also assesses a candidate's ability to be a team player: "If I hear that he or she owned his or her work, take psychological responsibility and pride, and talk about the team or the group, then it feels good to me. Too much reference to 'I' or not enough sense of accountability for the work effort says to me that this person is not really a team player."

Coates also believes you must meet with a candidate more than once to get a true read. "Sometimes the connection is instantaneous, but I always meet twice with a person if I am serious about them." Coates invites others to participate in the screening process. The interview "committee" may include "their potential peers, key clients and usually someone else on my management team that I believe has good interviewing and people skills." Having a candidate meet with multiple interviewers gives the primary hiring manager an opportunity to cross-check her own initial impression. Coates concludes, "Having a candidate meet with different interviewers helps validate or highlight something I may have missed. Project managers need to be able to work with a variety of people, so this helps assess their organizational fit."

Organizations must be willing to invest in staff and to build practical and emotional competencies. Human Resources can lend a supportive hand in the process, by encouraging staff to engage in some honest self-assessment. A 360-evaluation of performance, for example, is good for this purpose because it points out areas in which an individual may be challenged. Most individuals have difficulty recognizing areas of improvement for themselves; a mentor or advisor can help with this process.

Finding the "Right" Match

Hiring project managers who meet the technical and personality requirements and who "fit" with the company's culture is only half the battle. Matching the "right" project manager to the "right" project is equally grueling. Before assigning a project manager, quickly appraise the project's characteristics and match the requirements to the indi-

vidual who can best meet the global needs. Consider the following
questions before completing the assignment:

- Does this candidate have adequate experience in managing this
  type of project?

- Does this candidate have previous experience managing similar-
  sized projects?

- Is this candidate able to effectively manage a team this large?

- Does this candidate have balanced control over emotions? The
  ability to handle stress?

- Is this candidate ready for a bigger challenge?

- What level of self-awareness does this candidate hold in relationship management? Social awareness? Self-management?

The PMO plays a significant role in the matchmaking process—the
more successful the match, the more successful the outcome for everyone. Not repeating the same mistakes is key; this is just one example
of how collecting lessons learned adds value. Let's explore more about
lessons learned in the next chapter.

CHAPTER 10

LESSONS LEARNED

There are no mistakes or failures, only lessons.

Denis Waitley

What is Success?

Measuring project success goes beyond hitting project end dates. Most organizations that employ project management practice define success at the project level, meaning each project is individually evaluated on a number of measurable components to determine if the project ended "successfully" or not. This is a good place to start. However, organizations should apply a more global definition of success, one that extends beyond individual projects to include measures of how effectively the organization succeeded in meeting its strategic objectives.

All organizations should focus on two critical areas in defining success: the project level *and* the portfolio level. Questions to consider include:

1. Did we launch the "right" set of projects? Did the projects best support our goals? Did we meet our business outcomes? How does this information help inform us for next year's planning?

2. Did we manage projects "correctly"? Did we manage each project successfully? Did projects end on time? Can we improve in our project management practices to manage projects more efficiently?

Evaluating success requires honest, retrospective insight into both how the project was delivered and if the project delivered what it promised. The EPMO is obligated to lead their organization through this process, much as they guided the organization though the portfolio selection process. It requires discipline, facilitation, data collection, and an unbiased view. The results of the process must highlight both successes and failures to be effective.

Project Success—We Won't Be Fooled Again

Lessons learned are the nuggets of knowledge derived from past experience and outcomes to promote the reoccurrence of desirable results or prevent the reoccurrence of undesirable consequences.

Use of lessons learned is a principal component in project management methodology; it is a standard practice that enables organizations to reap knowledge from past project experience and apply that knowledge to current or future projects to avoid repetition of past failures. The practice is particularly valuable in organizations where current projects have components and attributes that are similar to previously managed projects (i.e., product development, IT, construction, etc.) While no project is identical to another, the collection and communication of lessons learned documentation is apt to save the next similar project or allow a project manager to more effectively manage a project. Let's focus first on the conventional practice of lessons learned.

Ideally, project managers should maintain a lessons learned log throughout the life of the project. This practice enables project teams to capture lessons learned as close as possible to the learning event. The log can be easily maintained by capturing a quick reference to the event, and by addressing the event in "real time" so projects do not become derailed. Another option is to capture lessons learned on a scheduled basis, such as at the start and end of each project phase.

Regardless of how and when lessons learned are captured and addressed, each project should also conduct a formal project closing exercise. A formal project closing is important to:

- Provide formal handoff to operations
- Obtain customer acceptance
- Communicate the end of the project
- Close off funding

- Release resources back to the organization
- Celebrate

Taking the time to conduct a lessons learned exercise is a good way to assess project efficiency. A PMO should always be looking for ways to motivate and encourage the act of formal project closing, as this formal practice allows a team to review project outcomes, capture lessons learned, and document results. Sharing the results with the PMO and other project teams enables continued project success, both by celebrating what worked well and warning others about what did not work as well as expected.

HPHC believes formalizing project closing activities supports three key functions: it captures key project metrics; reduces rework and pitfalls for future projects; and provides the opportunity to repeat what works well for projects.

Project closing is the process by which the project is brought to an end. The information from this practice is used to help improve the overall environment for project management in an organization. HPHC has designed a project closing statement (PCS) tool to support the project closing activities. The template provides four key elements:

- Project Closing Checklist—a reminder of the steps needed to close a project
- Project Completion—a place to document the project completion relative to expected project deliverables
- Business Success—a place to document the business success of the project relative to expected business outcomes
- Lessons Learned—a place to capture lessons learned for use by other projects at HPHC.

Let's examine each element of the project closing statement tool.

Project Closing Checklist

This section of the closing statement is meant to provide steps for the project manager to consider when closing a project. Project managers are supposed to check off areas to indicate completion:

- ❑ Complete handoff to operational units:
  - ○ Retain resources to support the transition
  - ○ Provide new process flows and other required documentation to operational units
  - ○ Provide metrics for all new processes
  - ○ Provide new/updated reporting schedule
  - ○ Obtain sign-off for handoff to operational units
- ❑ Obtain project sign-off from executive sponsor
- ❑ Communicate completion to all key stakeholders
- ❑ Conduct a post-project review meeting:
  - ○ Review accomplishments versus expected deliverables
  - ○ Complete project metrics (if possible at this time) to measure expected business outcomes
  - ○ Document lessons learned
- ❑ Complete final updates of the project schedule, status report, and project team list
- ❑ Submit completed project schedule, status report, and team list to PMO
- ❑ Archive project files:
  - ○ Store electronically on departmental server
  - ○ Provide inventory of archived files to PMO
- ❑ Celebrate and recognize the project team's efforts
- ❑ Prepare input to team members' performance appraisals
- ❑ Release all remaining resources
- ❑ Submit the Project Closing Statement to the PMO

Project Completion

The intent of this section of the project closing statement is to ascertain whether the project produced the anticipated deliverables when expected. The process includes revisiting the original project scope document, specifically focusing on the Deliverable, Completion Metric, and Planned Date sections, and then comparing each section, including the actual completion date and indicating if the deliverable was successfully provided by the planned date. Here is an example of how this may look:

ID	Deliverable (from POS)	Completion Metric (from POS)	Planned Date (from POS)	Actual Date	Successful (Y/N)
1					
2					
3					
4					
5					

Business Success

The purpose of this section of the project closing statement is to determine whether the project produced the anticipated business outcomes at the time expected. This is perhaps the most difficult phase, as business outcomes often cannot be measured until well after project closure. There are also instances where a project is launched without any known expected business outcomes, because none exist. This does not suggest the project was launched on a whim, but it does recognize that some projects are done simply because "it is the right thing to do." We'll discuss how to evaluate these types of projects later in this chapter. For now, let's focus on those projects that do contain valid business outcomes. Again, the process for capturing the information is simple;

it requires revisiting the original scope document and determining if the outcomes were met.

ID	Business Outcome *(from POS)*	Business Success Metric *(from POS)*	Expected Date *(from POS)*	Actual Date	Successful (Y/N)
1					
2					
3					
4					
5					

Lessons Learned

This is where honest reckoning occurs. It is perhaps the most difficult phase of the project closing activity, as it relies heavily upon team members' opinions and observations, as perceived through their eyes and experiences. The PMO can offer supportive guidance through this phase, by facilitating the process of identifying what worked and what did not. Soliciting this feedback from project team members can often be arduous for project managers for a variety of reasons. It can be burdensome for the project manager to solicit honest feedback from team members, particularly if the project faced challenges along the way. Team feedback places the project manager under a spotlight, one that will shine brightly to reflect good project manager leadership, but one that can be blinding when it focuses on project manager failure. Again, this feedback can be captured using a simple grid like this one to collect relevant data:

1. What Worked:

ID	What Worked? (Process, Tool, …)	Why Did It Work?	Suggestions for Improvement
1			
2			
3			
4			
5			

2. What Did Not Work:

ID	What Didn't Work? (Process, Tool, …)	Why Didn't It Work?	Suggestions for Improvement
1			
2			
3			
4			
5			

Case Study
The Vendor Fulfillment project utilized each section of the Project Closing Statement noted above. You will find details in the Appendix: *A Case Study.*

Some of what worked well for the Vendor Fulfillment team includes the following:

- The project team was assembled with the correct skills to do the work;

- Project team members' roles and responsibilities were clearly defined; and

- Meetings were productive.

Here are a few examples of what did not work well:

- User Acceptance Testing (UAT) experienced delays due to not enough resources being available when needed;
- Some vendors over-promised and under delivered; and
- Vendor selection delay should have re-calibrated the Go Live date.

Let the Form Be Your Guide

Forms and templates are a terrific way to collect information in a standard format. The standardization enables project teams to document project-closing activities according to a fixed system; it is a repeatable process that solicits key information in a predictable way. But be careful—collecting lessons learned according to a fixed set of components could also stymie honest and experiential feedback. Templates, particularly those for project closing, should always include a section to encourage free-form feedback. Find the right balance between methodical collection of important information without denying expression of a project team's true experiences.

Let the Liaison Guide the Process

Another way to further promote the sharing of important information is by using a facilitator to lead the project closing session. A PMO liaison is the perfect candidate for this role. Not only is the PMO liaison a neutral observer, she is also an informed witness, having supported the project, project manager, and project team from project inception to project closure. Like a guardian angel, the liaison has maintained protective oversight throughout the life of the project. What better person to facilitate a lessons learned session than one who knows enough about the project to ask good, probing questions, but who is not too close to feel responsible for things that may not have gone as planned. Since the PMO liaison has followed project activities since the beginning, the team is more likely to feel secure enough under the liaison's guidance to express honest feedback.

The project manager and liaison should set up a pre-planning meeting to establish the meeting strategy; identify the closing session agenda; establish roles (between facilitator and project manager); identify attendees; and agree on meeting ground rules.

Ground rules are important for making the most of the session. Some common ground rules may look like this:

- Express the importance of honest feedback

- Explain the feedback is *not* personal—remind participants to focus on the process to improve the process

- Limit criticism to constructive criticism

- All recommendations should be actionable

- This is not a decision-making session; it is to solicit feedback only

Other considerations when planning a session:

- Distribute materials in advance (meeting agenda, pre-filled in project closing document regarding project scope, etc.)

- Get feedback from those who cannot attend the meeting, ideally in advance of the session
  - o Provide a template for easy collection
  - o Offer to meet with them to hear their feedback directly

- Present the Project Completion and Business Success sections to the group as a whole
  - o Best to present this as a "review only" exercise
  - o Prominently display for group review and discussion (poster-size or on flip charts)

Collecting lessons learned is easy, with these few simple steps:

- Provide "categories for thought" to trigger the group
  - o Pre-fill in flip charts with categories to review
  - o Validate categories with attendees
- Brainstorm

- Ensure all participants are engaged (make everyone contribute)
- Follow the Rule of Threes
  - What worked/didn't work
  - Why did it work/didn't it work
  - Suggestions for improvement
- Prioritize suggestions at the end of the session
- Allow for anonymous feedback at the end of the session

It's also simple to document lessons learned:
- Distribute lessons learned documentation to participants as soon as possible
- Incorporate the lessons learned into the project closing document
- Store the information in the appropriate project document repository

Project Closing is For *All* Projects

Project closing activities must be conducted for all projects; it is the only way to truly assess and document successful project delivery. Project closings should occur for all projects, regardless of whether the project successfully closed or not. In some instances, a project will be shut down before it hits all deliverables; this can happen for a number of reasons, not always due to poor project management. Sometimes a business decision is made to stop a project before it is complete— this can be one of the most difficult decisions an organization must make, yet it may, in fact, be the best decision. When this happens, it is even more important to conduct a project closing session, because this type of project closure can be distressing and demoralizing to the team. A project closing is a perfect way for the team to reach proper closure before moving on. Be sure the rationale for project closure is well-communicated and lessons are shared among all stakeholders and customers.

Don't Keep It to Yourself

The Project Management Office is responsible for collecting lessons learned across the portfolio *and* for sharing the results with key stakeholders. When you have different projects with different people managing them, the same mistakes may be made without anyone recognizing it. Simply documenting results and storing them in a shared repository is not enough. The gems uncovered in lessons learned workshops are worth the PMO's investment in time spent scouring for and sharing results.

In many organizations, the PMO aggregates the results and assesses the need for enhancement to the project management methodology and training programs. This is the right approach for establishing a good continuous improvement cycle, but it needs more to become a great process. Evolving from good to great requires comprehensive scrubbing of data, multi-channel communication of results and findings, and interactive working sessions between project stakeholders.

HPHC's PMO recently expanded their model for collecting and storing lessons learned results, as the result of a big "a-ha!" moment. They recognized that project managers were diligent in conducting project-closing workshops and submitting lessons learned, and that project managers knew the EPMO was proficient in collecting the results and identifying opportunities for improvement and best practices. Yet, the light bulb came on when the PMO admitted the information was not being communicated back to the project management community in a real or actionable way. What good are lessons learned if you don't have a mechanism in place to shout "Danger!" when project teams are about to hit a pothole previously identified through another team's journey? Alternately, what good are gold nuggets of best practices if the wealth is not shared with others?

HPHC now conducts an annual "Lessons Learned Workshop" dedicated to sharing lessons learned from the previous year. All project managers and project leads are invited to participate in the two-hour session, which includes a summary report of lessons learned findings (as identified by the PMO's review of project closing documents), an opportunity for individual project managers to share specific best practices (as discerned through individual project experiences), and roundtable discussions (offering an occasion for participants to further explore their past project experiences relative to the findings). The session allows project managers to showcase their best practices with peers and promotes healthy discussion and debate, which would not normally occur if the audience were to simply read the findings in a report. The workshop enables people to really experience project team encounters in a real and meaningful way.

The annual workshop is a great way to bring project managers together, to celebrate accomplishments, and to share painful moments. This is a terrific way to further strengthen the project manager community; the event inevitably produces cheers of support and recognition when a best practice is shared—and heads always nod in sympathetic acknowledgement when a project manager reveals a difficult challenge.

Project managers will suggest their jobs are like no other in the organization, and in some instances, they do not always feel as recognized or valued as they would like. Maintaining a unified community for project managers is critically important—for the project managers *and* for the organization.

The results of the lessons learned workshop are presented to senior management. This important step maintains the link between the project stakeholders. Often, there is valuable feedback that warrants senior leader action. For example, some "actionable" feedback for HPHC senior leaders last year focused on two areas: the need to allocate resources to a project more quickly, and the need to define and follow an issue escalation process. Feedback from project teams can also improve the role of the executive sponsor; feedback often ranges from how the sponsor approves the project to how the sponsor oversees the project. Once again, the PMO is leveraged as the neutral party to effectively communicate findings and facilitate problem-solving.

Valuable Lessons

HPHC's annual Lessons Learned workshop highlights the injury and pain inflicted by certain offenders. Unfortunately, the usual set of suspects typically appears in the line-up each and every year—it's what we do (or don't do) with the suspects that makes a difference. For the past two years, HPHC project managers have identified opportunities for improvement in the following areas:

- Project Coordinator Positions
- Project (Core) Team Meetings
- Project Documentation
- Project Resources
- Project Management Practices
- Project Communications
- System Testing
- Risk Management
- Lessons Learned Practices

Let's spend a minute or two on each topic to understand how HPHC follows their simple formula for success:

Solution in Response to Problem = Success

Project Coordinator Position
Problem: Not enough project coordinators to adequately support project activities.
Solution: Assign project coordinators to multiple, similar projects simultaneously to gain efficiencies. Grow administrative staff to support project needs; share roles.

Project (Core) Team Meetings
Problem: Too many core team meeting requirements prevent project team members from accomplishing work.
Solution: Establish and schedule a regular meeting schedule for core team members and stick to it. If additional meetings are needed, try to conduct virtual meetings, use email exchanges, and leverage WebEx technology to efficiently share information without bogging down core team members with more (formal) meetings.

Project Documentation
Problem: Too much documentation, too few places to store and share pertinent information.
Solution: Use central repositories, use naming conventions, use change control/version control; establish ownership.

Project Resources
Problem: Too much dependency on specific individuals; never enough available resources.
Solution: Develop back-up/contingency plans for key personnel; establish development plans to grow content expertise.

Project Management Practices
Problem: Need standardized schedule layout; need joint planning process to synchronize initiatives; need to define and follow issues resolution processes; need to define and follow a decision process.
Solution: Create MSProject template sets; design focused training in decision-making, risk management, and document control processes. Revisit corporate decision-making model to insure it is still adequate and efficient.

Project Communication
Problem: Large programs require dedicated communications team with feedback loop to/from target audience; communications for change initiatives must happen early; e-mail messages tend to not be ready due to lack of interest or time.
Solution: Develop Communications Planning course; insert triggers and reminders for project teams to begin project communications from onset of project planning activities; leverage PMO Liaisons to help initiate communications planning earlier.

System Testing
Problem: Need more detail in testing specifications; not enough time to create/plan test scripts; inaccurate time estimates for testing, no time for iterations; test issues grids are needed to document/track descriptions, ownership and status of issues.

Solution: Investigate current processes—query project managers on testing to better understand how they derive their time estimates, what is their testing methodology; how can we improve? Initiate process improvements.

Risk Management
Problem: Too often risk management is done in a reactive mode instead of with proactive anticipation.
Solution: Design and conduct a proactive workshop regarding project risk (a "pre-mortem").

Lessons Learned
Problem: When is the "best" time to conduct a lessons learned session?
Solution: The ideal process produces continuous recording throughout the project lifecycle. The second-best option is to conduct the session immediately at the closure of a project phase, i.e., planning or testing. As a last resort, wait until the project closes. Leverage PMO Liaisons to monitor project activities and trigger reminders to the project team.

A Time for Reflection

We know the lessons learned workshops are important, because they allow project teams to pause and reflect on what worked well and what didn't before they move on to the next project. Project team members all need to reach full project closure before moving on. For project managers completing a large, complex, and long project, the formal process allows healthy reflection before they continue on to lead the next demanding project. Project team members also need to participate in closing activities, as many will return to their "real" jobs; the project closing process allows them to leave their hat at the project door before re-entering the world they left behind. There is a symbolic meaning to each project closing which should not be ignored. This is especially true if the project endured many complications.

The Boundaries of Success

True evaluation of success must extend beyond individual projects. It requires a comprehensive view of the project portfolio as a whole. This is where evaluation gets tricky. The portfolio contains many unique initiatives; all with varying start and end dates, different goals and objectives, and disparate deliverables. Some projects have interdependent relationships; others do not. The portfolio is a multiplex. Determining the success of a business plan and its associated initiatives represents many challenges. For example, many of the benefits from a project don't accrue until months or longer after project closing; it is critical to understand the expected results in terms of the overall business goals and when to anticipate real results. The approach to tracking and evaluating business plan results well after a project has closed is precarious because it demands ongoing evaluation of many moving parts, often well beyond the point at which the business plan ends.

Business plan success should be evaluated throughout the business cycle; organizations that wait until the end of the year to evaluate their ability to select the "right" projects, hit the "right" outcomes, and meet strategic goals will find themselves too late to take corrective action. Organizations must also pause at the end of each business cycle to evaluate their effectiveness in hitting the "right" targets to make strategic gains *before* they launch into the next business planning and portfolio building processes.

Senior leaders responsible for building the portfolio must know how they did with their project selections. They must know if the projects they identified as most likely to best support the strategic direction were actually successful. This analysis requires heavy emphasis on assessing a project's ability to meet expected business outcomes. A retrospective review of expected business outcomes helps senior leaders answer such key questions as:

- Did we hit our target outcomes?
- What could we have done differently to produce more favorable results?
- How do these results influence our process and/or decisions for next year?

HPHC has answered these questions by gradually introducing evaluation "gates" throughout the business planning cycle. The evaluation points focus on two areas: how to improve the overall business planning/portfolio building process and how to get better at evaluating successful business outcomes. Over the past year, HPHC's Business Oversight Committee (which is responsible for developing multi-year business plans and budgets to meet corporate goals) has gradually introduced methods to coordinate the implementation and monitoring of the plan's effectiveness. Their current metrics framework reflects their corporate responsibility; it is defined in three areas:

- Develop multi-year business plan
- Implement and monitor plan effectiveness
- Evaluate overall committee effectiveness

Today, HPHC's framework provides process and outcomes measures that evaluate corporate business plan development and execution:

	Process Measures	Outcomes Measures
Plan Development	• **Board of Directors approve business plan**	• **Retrospective review of business plan**
Plan Execution	• **Corporate Portfolio Executive Summary Report (Status red/yellow/green)**	• **Other performance measures against budget**

The PMO supports the committee's goal of implementing and monitoring the plan's effectiveness, as much of the data to support the outcome measures in this area is managed and maintained through PMO processes. The PMO collects and analyzes information to provide the business oversight committee with the ability to assess the results (business outcomes) of the selected projects, with the goal of better selection of the project portfolio and better project delivery (through an understanding of project expectations).

Over the course of 2006, HPHC's PMO conducted a pilot study on a select number of portfolio projects, focusing on two areas of study:

- Expected Business Outcomes
  - o Do we have defined targets?
  - o Did we hit our targets?
- Project End Date Changes
  - o Why do they change?

Expected Business Outcomes

The study evaluated business outcomes by reviewing a select number of project scope documents and comparing them to project closing statements to see if and how results may have changed in the time from original project launch to project closure. These findings suggest there was much variation across projects in how business outcomes were defined and documented. For example, some projects defined business outcomes by listing project deliverables, while in others, business outcomes were completely omitted. In other instances, the original business outcomes identified at project inception were completely different by project closing—sometimes for valid reasons, sometimes without explanation.

HPHC's PMO is currently addressing the issues identified through the pilot study with a focused action plan. They are:

- Creating specific guardrails to help define expected business outcomes for similar projects (i.e., product development, ROI, operational metrics)

- Designing and delivering focused training to project stakeholders on how to identify, declare, and document expected business outcomes

- Establishing an efficient process to collect, analyze, and present expected business outcomes findings in advance of succeeding business planning and portfolio building activities

Project End Date

The simplest and most common way to measure "project success" is to assess whether deliverables were completed on time. Thus, a common performance metric looks at whether projects ended "on time." Interestingly, many organizations do not take the time to adequately define the true project "end date," resulting in flawed data collection and analysis. Organizations must declare what the project "start date" is before defining the project end date. For example, does the project start at planning? Does the project start when all resources are secured? Does the project start when project status reporting begins? Does the project end when all project documentation is submitted? Or when the lessons learned wrap-up is conducted? What seems like a relatively simple metric may result in unanticipated complexities.

Be sure to define all start and end dates simply; communicate these definitions to all stakeholders so everyone knows how the project's success will be measured; and establish a simple system to collect and produce accurate data. The most important aspect of this process is creating the ability to capture actionable information—if you can't *do* anything with the data, why collect it?

For example, HPHC has seen an increased number of projects that have experienced end date adjustments—many projects over the past two years have extended their end dates by 30 days or more. The questions is why? Unless you have everyone defining project start and end dates consistently, how do you really know if the project is delayed or not? The sooner true project start/end dates are clearly declared and defined, the sooner a true analysis can be conducted to determine the root cause. When HPHC examined project start/end dates this year, they realized that not all projects experienced true delays—some projects simply declared start/end dates differently. Now that HPHC has set clear criteria to establish true start/end dates, they can examine how many projects really do extend their end dates—and why.

The Moral of the Story

Thoughtful contemplation is important. Taking time to pause and consider past performance is one of the best ways to anticipate the future. The PMO is obligated to continuously record and evaluate project management-related results and periodically revisit past organizational experiences—successes and failures—to determine how the PMO can offer ongoing value to the organization's success. The key to ongoing achievement is having the ability to balance the amount of time spent looking at the past against time spent anticipating the future. Then, you introduce processes and techniques to help guide the organization toward that future view vision.

As John F. Kennedy said, "Change is the law of life. And those who look only to the past or present are certain to miss the future."

No organization can afford to miss its future. Adopt simple project management practices today that will support your success tomorrow.

Appendix: A Case Study

Vendor Fulfillment Change
Project # O.29

Final Report
Deliverables Summary

Jim Thrasivoulos
October 2005

Table of Contents

Executive Summary

In 2004, Harvard Pilgrim Health Care's leadership committee approved the change of their fulfillment vendor in response to increased poor performance by their existing vendor. The project was added to the corporate agenda, and was sponsored by the Service Excellence & Operations Committee (SEOPS).

The journey began in October 2004, when request for information (RFI) proposals were sent to various vendors, including a late entry. The team evaluated all vendors. Vendor selection was based on RFI information, face-to-face vendor meetings, and the ability to meet HPHC's business requirements.

Vendor selection decision was delayed due to a major strategic decision, impacting the future of HPHC's operating system. HPHC's decision to replace its operating system introduced many project inter-dependencies, including Vendor Fulfillment. In April 2004, SEOPS and the Leadership committee approved the recommendation to partner with three fulfillment vendors:

- Vendor 1: Explanation Of Payments (EOPs)/Checks, Explanation Of Benefits (EOBs), Premium Bills, Negative Balance & Pending Provider Reports
- Vendor 2: Member Identification (ID) Cards
- Vendor 3: Post (Member) Sales Materials

A cross-functional team, involving representation from different business units at HPHC and the selected vendors, was formed to assist with the implementation of the fulfillment initiatives. Over the next five months, the fulfillment team accelerated implementation timelines and worked with the three selected vendors to review and understand HPHC business and technical requirements; establish service level agreements; re-design data files and reporting needs, negotiate pricing, establish Letter(s) Of Intent and Definitive Agreements, prepare marketing and benefit collateral for print-on-demand, design book covers, and address day-to-day issues during implementation.

The existing fulfillment vendor contract was set to expire on October 1, 2005, forcing the project team to perform under tight timelines. Limited resources and summer vacations added extra challenge to meeting production schedules. On September 12, 2005 the team successfully began approval for production activities in support of each initiative/vendor arrangement, starting with premium bills, Welcome kits, ID cards, EOBs and lastly, Provider checks and reports.

This report documents project deliverables, milestone implementation steps, and team decisions.

> **How to use this report**
> - The report is available in hard copy and through the PMO Project Reporting Database under Project O.29 Fulfillment Vendor Change
> - Each section of the report begins with a summary of the contents that follow.
> - The last section in this report references critical documents
> - Supplemental information is available on the Project Database. To access this information, follow the links found in the Report's Table of Contents.

Vendor Fulfillment Project—Business Opportunity

The project began in October 2004. The business opportunity was prepared and approved by SEOPS. Excerpts from the business opportunity statement follow:

Current vendor does not meet HPHC expectations:

1. 8 major initiatives with current vendor this year were late, jeopardizing business and cost objectives

2. 70% of UAT conducted by HPHC and not by current vendor due to "lack of trust" in their ability to perform

3. 68% of all current vendor management reports have errors and result in inability to tie weekly reports to actual production

4. Only 20% of invoices are received on-time or in correct format, resulting in difficult and time-consuming invoice reconciliation

HPHC has the opportunity to replace its current fulfillment vendor with vendor partner(s) that will provide the following benefits:

Current Opportunity- Internal (HPHC)	Current Opportunity-External (Members, Employers etc.)
1. Improve overall vendor fulfillment customer service (e.g., problem-solving production issues)	5. Improve overall vendor customer service (e.g., problem-solving production issues)
2. Reduce fulfillment cost by eliminating ID inventory stock by implementing print-on-demand (POD) technology ($60,000 ID cards; $90,000 contract)	• Improve post-sale kit presentation:
• Reduce the administrative complexity of the day-to-day management of invoicing, inventory and quality issues.	• Standardize order in which the existing items are presented within a kit
• Eliminate "exception processing" of kits as a result of current vendor(s) ability to meet all fulfillment requirements.	• Consolidate loose pamphlets into a single booklet
• Eliminate material inventory for post sales kits as a result of POD implementation.	• Build a foundation for personalizing kits
• Determine business owner for delivery of post-sale kits	
3. Create a centralized POD library for housing all current fulfillment material, which will reduce TAT for corrections and establish a system for version control.	
4. Expedite DOI delivery	

Future Opportunity-Internal (HPHC)	Future Opportunity-External (Members, Employers etc.)
• Provide strategic consulting services regarding industry best practices • Install new technologies or processes which are forward compatibility with HPHC 2005-2007 business plan • Outsource pre-sales kits (Phase II) • Consolidate all written communications to single vendor	• Install new technologies or processes which are forward compatibility with HPHC 2005-2007 business plan • On-line member access to print their own enrollment cards

The Fulfillment Vendor Project Team:

Vendor Fulfillment identified an Executive Sponsor, Project Lead and Project Manager early in the process, each with defined roles and responsibilities. The project team consisted of 24 HPHC staff and a variety of staff from external vendors. HPHC representation came from over ten different functional areas.

Business Owners:

Project leadership reviewed scope of work with management to identify business owners with an understanding that business owners will be responsible for requirements, decisions, UAT signoffs, and ultimately take ownership of the process after project closing.

The business ownership was established before the project was formally kicked off:

- Enrollment & Billing to own ID cards, post sale kits and premium bills.
- Member Services to own EOBs.

- Provider Relations to own EOP/Checks, Negative Balance & Pend Reports.

Core Team:

A core team was established to review progress, resolve issues and ensure milestones were delivered within their functional area of responsibility. The team met weekly to discuss project issues as well as participate with vendor weekly teleconferences. The core team consisted of ten cross-functional representatives.

Request for Information/Selection Process

As a follow-up to the original Vendor Assessment project, HPHC Business sent Request for Information/vendor quotes to six potential vendors:

HPHC Business reviewed the vendor responses and invited each of the vendors to meet the team, provide a capability presentation, and take part in a Q & A session. The RFI responses are archived in the PMO project database.

After the strategic decision regarding HPHC's future operating system was announced, additional screening considerations for developed for vendor candidates to insure vendors would meet the HPHC fulfillment requirements. Based upon RFI responses and new HPHC business needs, the project team focused on three specific vendors to ensure fulfillment requirements could be met. On March 15, 2005, the team presented and secured approval from the SEOPS Committee to engage with the three recommended vendors.

Business Requirements, Technical Requirements and Specifications

HPHC Business Requirements:

HPHC Business has developed (3) Business requirements for each of the vendor fulfillment initiatives:

1. ID Cards
2. Post Sales kits
3. Checks, EOPs, Negatives balances, Pend reports, EOBs and Premium Bills

The business requirements were pre-requisites to the Perot Systems IT technical requirements. Business requirements were reviewed and approved by the vendors. Business requirements and attachments are referenced in the definitive agreement and have been archived in the PMO database.

Perot Systems IT Requirements:

Perot Systems developed a set of requirements to implement file changes that needed to change to support new vendor implementation. Although the goal was to "lift and drop" the technical requirements from existing vendor to the new vendors, some files had to be converted from "print" to "data" because vendors could not accept print files (Design/flexibility constraints with print format).
     The following files required print to data file conversion:
   ❑ Checks
   ❑ Negative balances
   ❑ Premium invoices
   ❑ EOP calculations to the data file

Additional changes included:
   ❑ Added order number to the card/kit file for tracking purposes

Technical requirements and file layouts are stored in H:\Vendor Technical Specifications

Vendor #1 Technical Specification:

As part of client engagement, vendor #1 developed technical specifications to document the design logic for selecting benefit plan materials

(cc#s) from HPHC kit grid. The vendor also developed process documents including:
- ❑ Format guidelines for pdf submission
- ❑ Pull request forms
- ❑ Document submission, maintenance and approval
- ❑ Escalation process
- ❑ RRD Information Center and Audit Site

Specifications and process documents have been archived in the PMO Project Reporting database

Reporting Requirements

Vendor #1

Reporting requirements are documented in the PMO database. Reports include:
- ❑ Daily
  - o Data file receipt confirmation
  - o Audit report
  - o Reject audit reports: summary & detail
  - o Held record report: summary & detail
  - o HPHC special handling report
  - o Open enrollment report
  - o SOB & Face sheet acknowledgment report
- ❑ Weekly
  - o Inventory report
  - o Metrics on Volume and on-time
- ❑ Monthly
  - o Metrics on Volume and on-time
  - o UPS Mail Innovations invoice report
  - o Invoice report

Vendor #2

Vendor #2 hosts HPHC reports. The website is available and requires customer login. HPHC has been provided with user names and passwords for a number of HPHC staff. On-line reports can be downloaded to Enrollment & Billing Sequel database for analysis. The HPHC reporting requirements include:
- ❑ Daily
  - o Incoming file report
  - o ID card control totals
  - o ID card production detail reports
  - o ID card error detail report
  - o ID card return file log
- ❑ Monthly
  - o Production volume summary
  - o Production & Mail report
  - o Postage & Invoice report

Vendor #3

Vendor #3 uses a production system, Print Tracking and Reconciliation System (PTRS) that has on-line job tracking and reporting capability. The HPHC reporting requirements include:
- ❑ Weekly
  - o Incoming file report
  - o Check Accounting Page & Register with Special Handling Pieces
  - o Vendor weekly metrics report
  - o EOP File Verification Report
  - o Pend & Negative balance File Verification Report
  - o EOB File Verification Report
  - o Invoice File Verification Report

- Semi-Monthly
    - Postage & Invoice Report
- Monthly
    - Performance report (vs. SLA)

Vendor Planning Sessions

The project team invited each of the vendors to participate in vendor planning sessions. The project team used these sessions to:
- Reaffirm business proposition and assumptions
- Review business requirements and service level agreements
- Operating business models—new product and production
- Network Diagram (file transmission flow)
- Review projects plan (timelines and deliverable

Planning sessions enabled HPHC and vendor teams to evaluate requirement details and alternative options. Project goals and time-lines were re-affirmed.

Project planning sessions allowed the vendors to mobilize project teams, establish Q&A work sessions and work plans.

Each vendor submitted a project work plan. HPHC project manager worked with vendors to finalize plans and consolidated the vendor plans into the Vendor Fulfillment Integrated Schedule.

Following the planning work sessions, weekly conference call meetings were established with each of the vendors to review project status, milestones, and deliverables.

Service Level Agreements (SLA)

There are signed SLAs in place on quality, on time, and on responsiveness to issues with all three vendors. In addition, there are performance financial guarantees for the following services:

❏ **Vendor #1**

  o Premium bills late penalty fee—50% of operating cost for bills that do not meet the turnaround requirement (24 hrs for commercial cycles; 48 hrs for non-group and Medicare product cycles)

  o Premium bills quality—50% of operating cost and re-issue at vendor expense for bills that do not meet the correct invoice amount and are not mailed to correct group or member

  o Checks/EOPs and Negative Balance report late penalty fee—50% of operating cost for items that do not meet the turnaround requirement (File mailed on Sunday is processed and mailed by Tuesday). Special-handling checks are processed and received in WG by Tuesday

  o Checks/EOPs and Negative Balance report quality-50% of operating cost and re-issue at vendor expense for reports that do not meeting accurate amount, and are not mailed to correct payee.

❏ **Vendor #2**

  o ID card late penalty fee—50% of operating cost for cards that do not meet the turnaround requirement (Overnight & Performance guarantee cards: File received on Monday; produced and mailed on Tuesday; Standard processing cards are mailed on Wednesday)

  o ID card quality- Vendor to replace ID cards, with apology letter, at vendor expense

❏ **Vendor #3**

  o No financial penalties for post sale kits

Definitive Agreements/Letter of Intent (LOI)

Project leadership established a "two-way" contract relationship with each of the vendors. The "two-way" contract arrangement allows for better protection and ease of management.

Due to time constraints from the time we engaged with the three vendors, it was decided that a Letter Of Intent (LOI) for each vendor would be established to provide legal protection during the implementation. LOIs were drafted by HPHC's Legal Department. HPHC project manager/leader worked with vendors to finalize pricing, business requirements, and Service Level Agreements (SLAs). Each vendor signed the LOIs together with pricing, requirements, and SLA exhibits in July 2005.

Vendor #1 Statement of Work (SOW):

In addition to the HPHC-Vendor Business Requirement and SLA, a Statement of Work (SOW) was drafted by the vendor and was approved by HPHC business. The SOW and attachments document the scope of the work, SLA, and production procedures. The SOW is drawn up as part of the "contract."

Data Files:

The project goal was to "lift and drop" the existing data files from the exiting vendor to the new vendors. However, since some files were transformed to data files, Perot Systems IT made programming changes to the new data files (as mentioned in the earlier section). Folder H:\Vendor Specification contains the IT requirements, Design specifications, file layouts and samples.

Data Transfers:

Fulfillment data files are sent to vendors from the HPHC PGP server to the vendors via SFTP protocol. Each vendor receives the file(s), sends an acknowledgment to HPHC and proceeds with processing the file. If a problem arises, vendors are instructed to contact HPHC Help Desk where the call gets dispatched to the appropriate technical support person. Production files are sent to vendors' daily, weekly and monthly—depending upon file type.

User Acceptance Testing (UAT)

User acceptance testing was carried out by HPHC business. Initially, the project team worked with the vendors to approve the physical samples for each fulfillment initiative including:

- ❑ Vendor #1
  - o ID card layout & logo placement
  - o ID card carrier
  - o ID card inserts
- ❑ Vendor #2
  - o Marketing & EOC benefit document conversion
  - o Book cover
  - o Table of Contents
- ❑ Vendor #3
  - o Report samples (Check/EOP, EOB, Negative balances, Pend and premium bills)
  - o Text box/variable messaging

Upon approval of the samples, HPHC business developed test files that would allow reviewing output of various fulfillment scenarios:

- o ID Cards
- o Post Sales Kit
- o Checks/EOPs, EOBs, Negative Balance & Pend Reports
- o Premium Invoices

Project Communications

Corporate Reporting:
Weekly status reports were submitted to the PMO according to reporting requirements. All "Yellow" or "Red" reports were presented and discussed at senior leadership meetings.

Service Excellence & Operations (SEOPS) Committee:
Project updates were presented to the SEOPS committee at regular intervals. Updates included project accomplishments, schedule reviews, risk, concerns, and mitigation plan. SEOPS presentations are archived in the PMO project database.

Communication Plan:
The project team developed a plan on how to communicate the vendor change to constituents. It was decided that Corporate Communications would handle the external communications and coordination of the sales messaging.

Company-wide Communications:
Prior to production, the team presented to internal constituents/stakeholders including Sales and Member Services.

Vendor fulfillment project article was published in the HPHC *Wednesday Report.*

Expected Business Outcomes:
The project hit its projected ROI; current vendors continue to perform as expected and member satisfaction remains high.

Production:
New vendor fulfillment initiatives went into production as of September 2005. Project team established 24/7 Help Desk procedures for vendor support.

The project team monitored production runs and also managed production issues by working root-cause and preventative corrective action. The project team tracked initial production issues on a post-production issues report.

The project closed approximately 30 days post Go Live and as soon as operational hand-off was completed. The project hit its originally projected end date. Product change requests are now documented and reviewed by the HPHC Vendor Relations Specialist. Vendor estimates scope of work, timeline, and implementation cost.

Current Status:
ROI continues to run according to projections. Of the three vendors, vendor #1 did not consistently meet HPHC's service levels for turn-around time in 2006. This is perhaps due to a "special" request made by HPHC, which required this vendor to include a mailing insert with ID cards in May 2006. As soon as the insert requirement ended, the service levels returned to expectation. As a result, SLA penalties were applied to vendor #1 twice in 2005, 6 times in 2006, and once in 2007.

Vendor #2 has missed their service levels only once, in mid-September 2005.

Vendor #3 has never missed their mailing due dates since their Go Live date (mid-September 2005).

Case Study: Project Opportunity Statement

Project Name:	Fulfillment Vendor Change	Project ID:		O.29
Exec Leader:	Vicki Coates	Project Leader:	Corinne Orlinski	Project Manager:	Jim Thrasivoulos
Start Date:	10-5-04	End Date:	8-23-05	Date Submitted:	1-13-05

1. Business Opportunity:

Current vendor does not meet HPHC expectations:

- 8 major initiatives with current vendor this year were late, jeopardizing business and cost objectives

- 70% of UAT conducted by HPHC and not by current vendor due to "lack of trust" in their ability to perform

- 68% of all current vendor management reports have errors and result in inability to tie weekly reports to actual production

- Only 20% of invoices are received on-time or in correct format resulting in difficult and time-consuming invoice reconciliation

HPHC has the opportunity to replace its current fulfillment vendor with vendor partner(s) that will provide the following benefits:

Current Opportunity— Internal (HPHC)	Current Opportunity— External (Members, Employers etc.)

• Improve overall vendor fulfillment customer service (e.g., problem-solving production issues)
 	
 • Reduce fulfillment cost by eliminating ID inventory stock by implementing print-on-demand (POD) technology ($60,000 ID cards; $90,000 contract)
 	
 • Reduce the administrative complexity of the day-to-day management of invoicing, inventory and quality issues.
 	
 • Eliminate "exception processing" of kits as a result of current vendor(s) ability to meet all fulfillment requirements.
 	
 • Eliminate material inventory for post sales kits as a result of POD implementation.
 	
 • Determine business owner for delivery of post-sale kits
 	
 • Create a centralized POD library for housing all current fulfillment material, which will reduce TAT for corrections and establish a system for version control.
 	
 • Expedite DOI delivery
	• Improve overall vendor customer service (e.g., problem-solving production issues)
	
	 • Improve post-sale kit presentation:
	   1. Standardize order in which the existing items are presented within a kit
	   2. Consolidate loose pamphlets into a single booklet
	   3. Build a foundation for personalizing kits

Future Opportunity—Internal (HPHC)	Future Opportunity—External (Members, Employers etc.)
• Provide strategic consulting services regarding industry best practices • Install new technologies or processes which are forward compatible with HPHC 2005-2007 business plan • Outsource pre-sales kits (Phase II) • Consolidate all written communications to single vendor	• Install new technologies or processes which are forward compatible with HPHC 2005-2007 business plan • On-line member access to print their own enrollment cards

2. Project Goal:

Select, contract and implement with new fulfillment vendors. Bring on line with minimal business disruption.

3. Constituents:

☒ Members   ☒ Providers   ☐ Brokers   ☒ Accounts
☒ HPHC Employees   ☐ Other:

4. Scope:

4.1 Business Process Scope

In Scope	Out of Scope
Members: • ID card generation • Post Sales kit printing • Exception process of ID cards & kits • Generation of checks and invoices • EOBs • <u>Employers:</u> • Generation of invoices • <u>Providers:</u> • Generation of checks and invoices • EOP, Neg. Balances and Pends • <u>All:</u> • File formats and processing logic for data transfer	• Benefit content redesign • AMISYS coding, displays or language • Pre-sales kits (till Jan 06) • Returned EOP mail • Amisys Blue

4.2 Business Product Scope

In Scope	Out of Scope
• Commercial (including non-group) • FSEN (including non-group) • All States & products	

4.3 Organization Scope

In Scope	Out of Scope
Account Services	
Member Services	
Benefits Administration	
Corporate Communications	
CMAP (Central Administration)	
Enrollment and Billing	
Finance/AR & AP	
Network Services & Operations	
Perot Systems IT & Claims	
Sales	
Legal	

4.4 Application Software Scope

In Scope	Out of Scope
• SFTP server (File transfer to Vendors) • Web access for POD	•

4.5 Other Scope

In Scope	Out of Scope
•	•

5. Expected Business Outcome/Contribution to Corporate Goals—*Measuring Business Success*:

The following Business Outcomes are expected as a result of achieving the deliverables listed in the next section:

Corporate Goal (do not edit this column)	Expected Business Outcome Description / Contribution and Metric(s)	Expected Date
Grow to one million members by the end of 2007	Description: N/A Current Metric: Expected Metric:	
Meet or exceed our financial targets	Description: Cost reduction through POD implementation and new contract Current Metric: N/A Expected Metric: Reduction of $65,000 committed in 2005 budget, by reducing card stock to one (1) Description: Contract savings (2005 budget) Current Metric: N/A Expected Metric: $90,000 committed Description: Eliminate physical inventory management Current Metric: On-hand inventory 181,000 kit items Expected Metric: No preprinted items; Adobe files printed on demand in a pdf booklet (shell) Description: Vendor Service Level Agreement in-place; No internal fulfillment metrics	3/1/05

Corporate Goal (do not edit this column)	Expected Business Outcome Description / Contribution and Metric(s)	Expected Date
	Current Metric: Vendor reports monthly metrics: TAT Cards: 99.92% (24 hrs) TAT kits: 85% (48-hrs) TAT EOBs, EOPs Invoices, Pends: 100% (48 hrs) Production Standards: not available today Expected Metric: TAT Cards: 99.92% (24 hrs) TAT kits: 99.9% (48-hrs) TAT EOBs, EOPs Invoices, Pends: 100% (48 hrs) SLA will be in place Productions Standards: to be developed	
Develop an infra-structure for the future	Description: Develop electronic material library that enables vendor to print on demand. Current Metric: Current vendor cost for kits Expected Metric: Reduction in material handling costs and postage	*3/1/05*
Develop a high performance organization	Description: Current Metric	

6. Major Project Deliverables—*Measuring Project Completion*:

The following Major Deliverables will be completed during this Project:

Deliverables	Description/Completion Metric(s)	Planned Date
1. Document requirements	**Delivered when:** • Requirements complete (Business & IT) • Metrics defined • Statement of Work (SOW) complete	*01/15/05*
2. Award vendor fulfillment contract	**Delivered when:** • Contract bid complete • RFIs received and reviewed • Recommendations made • Letter of Intent initiated • Contract and SLA signed	*2/1/05*
3. Vendor implementation plan received	**Delivered when:** • Kickoff meeting complete • Vendor Account team established • Project plan complete • Schedule complete	*2/15/05*
4. Vendor build & test	**Delivered when:** • Vendor process development complete • Product test complete • Test samples complete	*6/2/05*
5. Run UAT	**Delivered when:** • Test scenarios & scripts complete • UAT runs scheduled • UAT complete	*8/1/05*

Deliverables	Description/Completion Metric(s)	Planned Date
6. GO- Live	**Delivered when:** • Production runs complete	*8/22/05*
7. xisting vendor contract review	**Delivered when:** • Decision secured	*2/1/05*
8. Operational Handoff	**Delivered when:** • Fulfillment process documented • Performance measures/ reviews established • Business owners sign off	*8/31/05*
9. Project closing	**Delivered when:** • Workshop complete	*8/31/05*

7. Major Milestones—*What it takes to get us there:*

The following Major Milestones must be met during this project:

Milestones (e.g., Capital Budget Approved)	Measure of Milestone (e.g., Capital Budgeting Committee signed off on project request)	Planned Date
Presentation to SEOPS	**Completed when:** • Presentation complete • SEOPS approval	10/12/04
Project Initiation Workshop complete	**Completed when:** • PIW complete • POS revised • Resources committed	10/14/04
Project Opportunity Statement complete	**Completed when:** • Submitted and approved by SEOPS	10/12/04

Milestones (e.g., Capital Budget Approved)	Measure of Milestone (e.g., Capital Budgeting Committee signed off on project request)	Planned Date
Project Planning Workshop	**Completed when:** • PPW complete • Project schedule developed • Resources committed	10/18/04
Project schedule	**Completed when:** • Project plan published & approved	10/29/04
Document requirements	**Delivered when:** • Requirements complete (Business & IT) • Metrics defined • Statement of Work (SOW) complete	2/1/05
Assess additional vendors	**Completed when:** • Vendor RFI received and reviewed • Financial/ Capability analysis complete • Recommendations complete	10/30/04
SEOPS presentation	**Completed when:** • Vendor recommendations presentation complete	11/2/04

Milestones (e.g., Capital Budget Approved)	Measure of Milestone (e.g., Capital Budgeting Committee signed off on project request)	Planned Date
Award Vendor contract	**Completed when:** • Pricing complete • SLA in-place • Statement of work complete • Contract and SLA negotiated and signed	2/1/05
Vendor implementation plan received	**Delivered when:** • Kickoff meeting complete • Vendor Account team established • Process requirements review complete • Specifications complete • Project plan complete	2/15/05
Conduct 2nd PPW with Vendor(s)	**Delivered when:** • PPW with vendor complete • Project schedule complete	11/18/04
Run UAT	**Completed when:** • Requirements complete • Products identified for library • IT requirements (web interface established) • Test run complete	8/1/05

Milestones (e.g., Capital Budget Approved)	Measure of Milestone (e.g., Capital Budgeting Committee signed off on project request)	Planned Date
Go Live	**Completed when:** • Milestones phases complete • Operating procedures complete • Report samples complete • Test runs complete • Production run	5/1/05
Operational Handoff	**Completed when:** • Process changes documented • QC/ Procedures established • Staff trained • Business owner signs off • Business leader notified of handoff	8/31/05
Terminate contract with Standard Register	**Completed when:** • Contract terminated	
Conduct project closure	**Completed when:** • Project closing workshop complete • Project working statement complete	8/31/05

8. Committee Approvals

☐ Product Development Leadership Team (PDLT)
☒ Service Excellence Operations (SEOPS)
☒ Capital Budget Committee (CBC)
☐ E-Architecture Steering Committee
☒ Information Technology Planning Committee (ITPC)
☐ Provider Medical Cost Team (PMCT)
☐ Decision Support & e-Health Plan Lead Team (DELT)
☐ Other:

9. Assumptions:

- Select vendor(s) by 10/25/04
- Sign contract by 10/30/04
- Handling EOBs for HDHP new product- Requirements complete by 11/1/04

10. Risks to Project and Contingency Plans:

Risk	Contingency Plan
• Resources from key areas are available as required	•
• Resource contention with the CASR project	•
• Disruption of 4/1/05 small business renewal process	•
• Delay of business requirements from Periodic Assessment team could impact go-live for HDHP	•
• Ability of new vendor(s) to implement according to plan	•

11. Dependent Initiatives:

This project is relying upon: (Project cannot be completed unless this work is done)	This project is necessary for: (Project results will contribute to these projects)
• HDHP EOB procedure	• Periodic statement assessment
• IT to establish Web interface	•
• Branding strategy	•
• Segmentation strategy	•

Describe any impact this project will have on the Core Administrative Replacement initiative:	Describe any impact the Core Administrative Replacement initiative will have on this project:

12. Core Team Personnel Resources:

Business Unit	Skill Set / Function	Resource Name	Role and Responsibility
E & B	Card requirements/ acceptance		Business/ IT requirement definition Metrics development Production
Corporate Communications	Post-Sales kit POD requirements/ acceptance		Kit POD development
BA	Vendor Mgmt POD definition/		Business requirements POD Kits, Benefit administration Performance metrics
HPHC IT	IT Project Mgr		IT Project Management
CMAP	Consulting		Consulting
FP & A	Financial analysis		RFI financial analysis Vendor selection
Finance	AR/ Invoicing		Premium invoices requirement definition
Corp Accounting	Accounts Payable		
Perot IT	Project Mgmt		Project Management

Business Unit	Skill Set / Function	Resource Name	Role and Responsibility
Perot IT	Claims Cards, Kits Business requirements Business requirements		Business reqts, code, test Business requirements development
Claims Services	Claims reporting		Requirements
Acct Services	Consulting		Consulting
Member Services	Consulting		
Net Svcs	Consulting		Provider Relations Business requirements—Provider
Legal	Contract review		Contract review Vendor selection
Treasury	Treasury		Consulting
PMO	Project facilitation/ reporting	Ron Parello	Consulting
Ops Intg	UAT		UAT
OPS/ Intg	Project Mgr.	Jim Thrasivoulos	Project Management
HPHC IT	IT Project Leader		Project leadership, Risk assessment
BPO	Business Project Leader		Project leadership, Risk assessment
BPO	Executive Project Leader		Consulting

14. Financial Analysis:
See Initial analysis presented to SEOPS on Oct 5, 2004
Final analysis due by Oct 30, 2004

15. Authorization to Proceed:

_____

Date
Executive
(TLC Member)

_____

Chief Operating Officer (COO)   Date

Case Study: Example of RAID

RAID Codes: Risks (R), Assumptions (A), Action Items (AI), Decision (D) Issues (I), Constraints

Subteam Codes: Core (C), Vendor (V), Legal (L), UAT (U)

sort by "date closed", then "date due", then

#	RAID Code	Sub Team	DESCRIPTION	DD DATE	OWNER	ACTION TO BE RESOLVED	DATE	Result	DATE
64	D	C	Business requirement changes: 1) Include pdf images back to HPHC and 2) Member EOP mailings will NOT be	05/24/0	Jim Y/ Bob	JimT to update business A to set up process of pdf file from FTP, index and sent to Cold in a timely	05/31/0	Complete	
62	AI	C	Postage & invoice	05/24/0	JimT/Sue B. Clare	Need to review vendor's postage and determine requirements	05/31/0	Reference	
61	AI	C	RRD on line	05/18/0	Core	5/18 Web demo were pricing has been received. Need to and decide on audit & requireme	05/31/0	Documented the line services HPHC will purchase Softproofi	
58	AI	C/V	RDeard turnaround times PSI will performance guarantee -day	05/12/0	Steven	Provided acct information & escalated to Customer Service.	05/18/0	5/23: Decision made to go with teslin. Vendor will support requireme	
56	AI	C	Vendor needs signatures & logos from	05/09/0	Cindy	Cindy to	05/10/0		
49	D	C	Confirm magnetic stripe decision on	05/05/0	Jim	Review HPHC position with Chris	05/12/0	No Magnetic stripe on ID cards initial phase. Space can be used	
47	AI	C	Critical path item: Initial data files requested by not be ready when needed. (premium bills, EOBs, Pends & Negative	05/04/0	Bob A/ Jim	Review schedule and establish DPS can receivees"	05/16/0	Bob A to deliver "mockup" test (identical format) and send to needle	

Project Status Report—Sample

Project Status Report	Summary Update:	PMPL Status
as of: August 12, 2005	Project remains on yellow because of Perot IT test file integrity issues and ID card artwork (logo issues) not been approved. UAT underway for ID cards, EOP/ Checks and Negative Balance reports. Completed 1st test run for Premium Bills. Complete project transition planning from existing vendor to new fulfillment vendors and established project communication plan.	Y

Project ID:	0.29	Project Name:	Fulfillment Vendor Change		
Exec. Leader:		Project Leader:		Project Manager:	Jim Thrasivoulos
Project Goal:	Select, contract and implement with new fulfillment vendors using a conversion strategy. Bring on line with minimal business disruption.			Project Start:	10/15/2004
				Project End:	10/1/2005

Recent Activities/Accomplishments:
1. ID card UAT on-going
2. Began EOP, Check, Neg Balance UAT
3. Incorporated Premium Bills changes from UAT run
4. Working on resolving technical issues with the integrated claim files
5. Finalized communication plan
6. Established transition plan
7. Reviewed and redlined vendor definitive agreements

Upcoming Events:
1. Complete 1st cycle of ID card UAT
2. Complete test output review of EOP, Checks, Neg Balances
3. Begin UAT premium bills (2nd run)
4. test files and Cold Storage
5. Review vendor bound kits (1st run)
6. Submit vendor redlined agreements
7. Vendor agreement review

Status Legend: G = as planned; Y = corrective action being taken; R = senior management attention required

Major Milestones:	Baseline	New Est.	Var	O/C	GYR	Risk Key
1 Vendor POS complete	4/7/2005	4/7/2005	0	C	G	
2 Vendor selection approved	3/29/2005	3/29/2005	0	C	G	
3 Existing vendor contract extension to 10/1/2005 completed	2/4/2005	2/4/2005	0	C	G	
4 Project schedule finalized	6/16/2005	6/27/2005	11	C	G	
5 Business requirements signed (by vendor)	5/20/2005	7/13/2005	54	C	G	
6 Letter of Intent signed (3)	5/23/2005	7/13/2005	51	C	G	
7 Fulfillment contracts signed (3)	8/15/2005		####	O	G	
8 IT requirements signed	12/1/2004	1/25/2005	55	C	G	
9 Technical specifications complete	2/14/2005	2/28/2005	14	C	G	
10 Code & IT Test- Amisys (All initiatives)	6/16/2005	6/16/2005	0	C	G	
12 Data connectivity requirements complete	6/17/2005	6/17/2005	0	C	G	
13 UAT test plan complete (All initiatives)	6/16/2005	6/16/2005	0	C	G	
14 Kit cover design, collateral, artwork & documentation submitted	5/31/2005	6/22/2005	22	C	G	
15 Printing For Systems- ID card samples approved	7/15/2005			O	Y	
16 ID cards UAT complete	7/29/2005			O	Y	
17 Vendor- Kit generation complete	8/1/2005			O	G	
18 Kits UAT complete (3rd test run)	8/24/2005			O	G	
19 Vendor- EOB,P,Checks, Premium Bills & reports generated	8/24/2005			O	Y	
20 UAT- EOB,P,Checks, Premium Bills & reports complete	8/24/2005			O	G	
21 Go live- ID cards	8/21/2005		####	O	Y	
22 Go live- Kits	8/31/2005		####	O	G	
15 Go Live EOB,P, Checks, Premium bills & reports	9/12/2005			O	Y	
16 Project Closing Statement Submitted (w/ Performance Measures)	10/1/2005			O	G	

Major Risks/Issues:	Mitigation/Action:	Back to "G"
A Vendor integrated test files experiencing integrity issues	Escalated within Perot IT- Daily status meetings w/ vendor & PerotIT	
B Vendor ID card logo placement issue	Escalated within vendor Management	

Project Closing Statement—Sample

Project closing is the process by which the project is brought to an end. The information from this template will be used to assist in improving the overall environment for project management in the organization. The Project Management Office will update the tools based on this information and provide a central place for accessing the lessons learned across all projects.

The **Project Manager should guide the team members and other stakeholders through a standard project closing process** *so that all projects are completed in an organized and successful manner. Project closing ensures that the loose ends are addressed and provides a mechanism for documenting and sharing lessons learned.*
This template provides the following sections:

- *Project Closing Checklist—a reminder of the steps needed to a close a project*
- *Project Completion—document the project completion relative to the expected deliverables*
- *Business Success—document the business success of the project relative to the business outcomes*
- *Lessons Learned—document lessons learned for use by other projects at HPHC.*

Project Closing Checklist:

The following checklist is meant to provide steps for the Project Manager to consider when closing a project. **Click on the check box** *to indicate completion:*

☐ Complete handoff to operational units:

   ☐ Retain resources to support that transition

   ☐ Provide new process flows and other required documentation to operational unit

   ☐ Provide metrics for all new processes

☐ Provide new/updated reporting schedule

☒ Obtain sign-off for handoff to operational units

☐ Obtain project sign-off from Executive Leader

☐ Communicate completion to all stakeholders

☐ Conduct a post-project review meeting:

  ☒ Review accomplishments versus expected deliverables

  ☐ Complete project metrics (if possible at this time) to measure expected business outcomes

  ☒ Document lessons learned

☒ Complete final updates of the project schedule, status report, and project team list

☒ Submit completed project schedule, status report, and team list to PMO

☒ Archive project files:

  ☒ Store electronically on departmental server

  ☐ Provide inventory of archived files to PMO

☒ **Celebrate**, recognize the project team's efforts

☐ Prepare input to team members' performance appraisals

☐ Release all remaining resources

☒ Submit the Project Closing Statement to the PMO

Project Completion:

As specified in the Project Opportunity Statement (POS), **the deliverable statements define what constitutes project completion**. *The purpose of this section is to ascertain whether the project produced the deliverables expected at the time expected.*

Copy the information for the Deliverable, Completion Metric, and Planned Date columns from the corresponding columns in Section 4 of the POS and complete the Actual Date (if the deliverable was provided) and a Y/N to indicate if the deliverable was successfully provided by the planned date.

ID	Deliverable (from POS)	*Delivered* **Metric** (from POS)	Planned Date (from POS)	Actual Date	Successful (Y/N)
1	**Business & Technical Require-ments complete**	• Develop business and technical requirements for each initiative (ID cards, Post Sale kits, EOP/Checks, EOBs, Premium Bills, Negative Balances and Pend reports • Review with business own-ers and Perot IT • Review Requirements with Vendors and Negotiate	2/1/05	2/1/05 6/10/05	Y[1]
2	**Award vendor fulfillment contract**	**Completed when:** • Pricing complete • SLA in-place • Statement of work complete • Contract and SLA negoti-ated and signed	2/1/05	3/31/05 6/10/05 6/30/05 Oct	Y[2]

ID	Deliverable (from POS)	*Delivered* Metric (from POS)	Planned Date (from POS)	Actual Date	Successful (Y/N)
3	Vendor implementation plan complete	**Delivered when:** • Kickoff meeting complete • Vendor Account team established • Project plan complete • Schedule complete	2/15/05	5/16/05 5/30/05	Y
4	Vendor Build & Test	**Delivered when:** • Vendor process development complete • Product test complete • Test samples complete	6/2/05	8/1	Y[3]
5	Run UAT	**Delivered when:** • Test scenarios & scripts complete • UAT runs scheduled • Samples approved • UAT complete	8/1/05	9/12/05	Y[3]
6	Production runs complete	**Delivered when:** • Production runs complete	8/22/05	9/18/05	Y

ID	Deliverable (from POS)	*Delivered* Metric (from POS)	Planned Date (from POS)	Actual Date	Successful (Y/N)
7	**Existing vendor contract review**	**Delivered when:** ❑ Decision secured	2/1/05	2/1/05	Y[4]
8	**Operational signoff**	**Delivered when:** ❑ Fulfillment process documented ❑ Performance measures reviews establish ❑ Business owners sign off	10/1/05		Y[5]

[1] Business and Technical requirements were approved internally but were held up until Vendors were selected (May 2005)

Time delay attributed to Management decision of CASR announcement and change original selected vendors

Due to CMS review requirements, FSEN product management removed FSEN kits from the scope of this project (e.g., consolidation of loose pamphlets into a bound book).

[2] Vendor recommendations were made to SEOPS on 3/31/05 based on pricing and RFI response. New vendors were announced following CASR. Fulfillment team began working with new vendor (SLA/business requirements review) on 4/12/05. Due to the contract complexity posed with CASR, Letters of Intent (including Requirements, SLA and pricing) were signed by the vendors

[3] There were (2) build and test cycles:

    1) Amisys surround code changed to support file conversion from print to date for checks, negative balance reporting and premium invoices. This was necessary to provide the flexibility the

vendors required. Perot IT performed coding and testing. There were additional requirements for the new files (documented in the Technical Requirements section in the PMO database)

2) The three vendors also built and tested their program and provided test output to HPHC for UAT

[4] Existing contract was extended to October 1, 2005

Business Success:

As specified in the Project Opportunity Statement (POS), **the expected business outcomes are the criteria by which the business success of the project will be determined.** *The purpose of this section is to ascertain whether the project produced the business outcomes expected at the time expected.*

Note that some business outcomes may not be measurable until a later time. The Executive Leader for this project is responsible for ensuring that the business outcomes are measured. The PMO will track this information and provide a reminder at the appropriate time.

Copy the information for the Business Outcome, Success Metric, and Expected Date columns from the corresponding columns in Section 2 of the POS and complete the Actual Date (if the business outcome was achieved) and a Y/N to indicate if the business outcome was successfully provided by the expected date.

ID	Business Outcome (from POS)	Business Success Metric (from POS)	Expected Date (from POS)	Actual Date	Successful (Y/N)
1	Meet or exceed our financial target	❑ Cost reduction through Print On Demand implementation and new contract. Reduction of $65,000 (committed in 2005 budget) by reducing card stock to one (1) ❑ Contract savings (2005) budget $90,000 committed ❑ Eliminate physical inventory (Current metric: 181,000 kit items; Expected metric: No preprinted items except cover) ❑ Vendor SLA in place (Current metric: No performance measures with financial penalty; Expected Metric: SLA with financial penalties	3/1/05		Y[1] Y[2] Y[3] Y[4]

ID	Business Outcome *(from POS)*	Business Success Metric *(from POS)*	Expected Date *(from POS)*	Actual Date	Successful (Y/N)
2	Develop an infra-structure for the future	Develop electronic material library that enables vendor to print on demand	3/1/05	10/1/05	Y[5]

[1,2] Project anticipates to reduce fulfillment cost due to print on demand initiatives. IT/Operations Accounting to track fulfillment cost as the new vendors began production on 9/18/2005. The negotiated prices with the new vendors are estimated to produce annualized savings of $360,000 from those of existing vendor beginning 10/1/2005

[3] HPHC benefit and marketing material adobe acrobat pdfs have been converted by vendor in a "print-ready" format. Book covers is the only stock items.

[4] Vendor SLAs includes financial performance penalties on turnaround times and quality for Checks/EOPs, ID cards and Kits

[5] Vendor has established electronic library to manage HPHC changes to the kits. As a first step, vendor has also added name personalization to the Welcome letter

Lessons Learned:

The information in this form can be collected at a post-implementation meeting of the project team and can provide help to future project teams working on similar projects. Invitees should include anyone who participated in the project at any time during the duration of that project. Each participant should come ready to provide input on what worked and what didn't work during the project. Suggestions for improvement should always be provided for 'didn't work' items.

1. What Worked:

ID	What Worked? (Process, Tool, ...)	Why Did It Work?	Suggestions for Improvement/ Recommendations
1	• Vendor technical specifications & process documentation	Vendor documented the programming logic and business rules that interprets the post sale kit grid into building the book. Process documentation established clear criteria for submission, engagement guidelines and version control. This documentation establishes a baseline and future changes.	Require other vendors to provide similar documents
2	• Project team was assembled with the correct skills to do the work	PM worked with project leadership and identified business owners and team members during the PIW	Identify and secure critical resources when needed (Team did not have adequate UAT resources in the timeframe needed)

ID	What Worked? (Process, Tool, ...)	Why Did It Work?	Suggestions for Improvement/ Recommendations
3	• Centralized kit library allows for fast correction	Process has been established to submit and revise documents. On-line services (soft-proofing) is available for quick approvals.	
4	• Everyone liked kit cover design	Held design review meeting. Vendors communicated production efficiencies and cost alternatives to Corp Communications at an early stage	
5	• Roles and responsibilities were clearly defined	Business initiative owners and project team skill levels were identified upfront. Clear roles and responsibilities made it easy to assign tasks and issues.	

ID	What Worked? (Process, Tool, …)	Why Did It Work?	Suggestions for Improvement/ Recommendations
6	• Meetings were productive	Stick to publish agenda. Used internal RAID reports, activity time-lines and vendor action registers to focus on the work	• Use project coordinator • 3 Concurrent vendor implementations required multiple weekly meetings (1 for each vendor and 1 core team) • During UAT, daily calls were held for each sub-team • Agendas, meeting minutes became difficult to prepare and manage
7	• Security was set up correctly	Use of dedicated network VPNs eliminated data exchange security risks	

Lessons Learned (continued):

2. What Did Not Work:

ID	What Didn't Work? (Process, Tool, …)	Why Didn't It Work?	Suggestions for Improvement
1	• Business requirement template	Wrong format—preformatted	Create project specific requirements template

ID	What Didn't Work? (Process, Tool, ...)	Why Didn't It Work?	Suggestions for Improvement
2	• IT specs	• Contracting with vendors late, prevented team to finalize technical specs. This forced subsequent activities to go to a "hurry-up" mode (coding, vendor programming, UAT) • Existing project work was handled by outside consultants. Technical documentation was not available for use. Programming logic was re-created to support printàdata file conversions	• Negotiate Stand Register contract longer than 6 months. • Project deliverables must be archived in a public folder for future use.

3	• UAT	• Not enough resources available when needed
		  o Unexpected illness
		  o Vacations
		  o Unable to secure business resource with UAT skills for vendor initiative
		• Problems with test environment (build)
		  o Slow to generate test files
		• UAT consisted of manual inspection of reports
		  o Missed item that surfaced into a provide problem (post date on EOP report; truncated address on a pend report)
			• Build slack-time during summer months (Jul-Aug) to compensate for vacations
			• Test environment constraints & resources must be reserved for each project
			• Seek UAT automation to prevent human inspection errors

ID	What Didn't Work? (Process, Tool, …)	Why Didn't It Work?	Suggestions for Improvement
4	• Vendor over-promised and under delivered	• Ran into problems with vendor on: o Meeting turnaround times for ON card packages, o Inserts o Logo placement on ID cards and logo alignment o Fonts o Flexible with ID card packages (Use of 1 card, 2 card or 4 card package combinations for family cards issued)	• Early on-site production assessment to confirm vendor capabilities • Build work relationship to work out technical issues
5	o Cover specs	Specs for the cover were written into the contract without consulting designer	o Review technical content of contract with appropriate subject matter experts
6	o Go live date	Vendor selection delay should have re-calibrated the go live date	In lieu of the vendor selection delay, existing vendor contract renewal should have been negotiated for longer than 6 months

ID	What Didn't Work? (Process, Tool, ...)	Why Didn't It Work?	Suggestions for Improvement
7	o Too many meetings/ preparation	Back-to-back meetings did not allow time to prepare	Agendas should be published 24-hrs in advance
8	o Vendor audits	Poor scheduling and cost constraints	Site visit/ process review should be completed before go live (preferably during requirements review)

About the Author

©Days End Photography

Lisa DiTullio, renowned speaker, is the director of the project management office (PMO) at Harvard Pilgrim Health Care, the #1 Health Plan in America, according to the U.S. News & World Report/NCQA America's Best Health Plans list. Her philosophy for simplicity has gained global recognition. Lisa lives in Boston with her husband and blended family of five children. She enjoys running and home renovation in her free time.

978-0-595-46110-3
0-595-46110-7

Printed in the United States
204805BV00001B/136-207/A

9 780595 461103